HAPPINESS, ANXIETY, AND WRITING

Using Your Creativity To Live A Calmer, Happier Life

L. M. LILLY

Writing As A Second Career

WHAT'S ANXIETY GOT TO DO WITH WRITING?

T. S. Eliot said that anxiety is the handmaiden of creativity.

I don't know if that's true for everyone. But as I struggled with anxiety, I realized that the skills and habits I'd developed as a writer often made it harder to live a calm, happy life. The habit of imagining the worst possible thing that could happen next, for instance, and then coming up with more and more terrible things is fantastic for plotting a suspense novel.

For real life, not so great.

To make it worse, writers usually spend a lot of time thinking and writing alone, without other people or activities to interrupt or distract us. And our love for writing often makes us less physically active. In fact, the acronym BICHOK (butt in chair, hands on keyboard) is often cited as the mantra for success. That, too, can increase anxiety and unhappiness.

But there's good news. It's not a one-way street.

Your creativity, imagination, and writing skills can be used to make your life richer and happier and ease your anxiety. This book shares what I've learned about doing exactly that and, I hope, will help you find the way to rewrite your own life.

MY STORY

I didn't start out a worrier. Just the opposite. I was a pretty happy, relaxed kid.

But as I grew to adulthood anxiety took hold. It reached a tipping point in my mid-twenties when I moved from Chicago to Los Angeles with my boyfriend, an aspiring screenwriter. He wanted to be where the film industry was.

Six months later I was in debt, unemployed, in pain, and living with my parents again. I remember lying awake listening to their cuckoo clock go off every single half-hour every night, my thoughts racing.

While in California, I'd worked a job where I typed 90 words a minute 8 hours a day at a bad keyboard set up. I developed a repetitive stress injury, something about which there wasn't a lot of understanding at the time. My hands, arms, and wrists ached and tingled and my little fingers on both hands went numb during the night.

The medical advice was to wear braces, keep working until it was bad enough for surgery (which back then involved cutting into your arms and wrists), and then do it all again in an indefinite cycle of work, injury, surgery.

That seemed like a phenomenally bad idea to me.

Everything I did for work or at which I hoped to work someday – writing, playing guitar, and word processing – hinged on my being able to use my hands. With my boyfriend unable to support us both, and a B.A. in Writing/English that didn't qualify me for much of anything, I moved home to my parents' house in Chicago.

I'd lost everything that mattered to me. And I felt like a failure.

My mom had barely spoken to me since I'd moved in with my boyfriend a few years before. (These were different times and living together without being married was still outside the norm.)

She unwittingly reinforced my feeling that I'd failed by telling me it was all God's plan so I'd stop "living in sin."

Full of anxiety and steeped in depression I obsessed over what I'd done to cause all of this and how horrible everything would be if I could never support myself again. Some days I could barely get out of bed.

Within a year, though, I'd retrained and gotten a job as a paralegal. (No typing required.) Within 2-3 years I'd learned ways to manage my condition. These days I only occasionally experience pain in my hands, wrists, and arms though I write a lot, and rarely have tingling or numbness.

The intense anxiety, though, plagued me on an off for decades, including when I later went to law school and after I achieved a fair amount of success as a lawyer. For years I was embarrassed to admit to anyone but my closest friends how much I struggled with it.

Happily, that's not my life now.

WHAT YOU'LL FIND INSIDE THESE PAGES

Part 1 of this book covers how many of us get stuck in a pattern of anxiety. Some chapters relate directly to writing, such as asking *What If* the worst possible thing happens (Chapter 2). Others are more general.

In Part 2 I'll talk about ways to rewrite our inner lives. These methods include derailing anxious thoughts and taking small steps to feel better before we try to deal with our fears. I'll also talk about changing our words (including questions we ask and how we describe ourselves and our lives). Part 2 ends with ways to deal with fears specific to writing.

Part 3 moves on to ways we can redesign the world around us.

Because anxiety isn't always solely in our heads. Sometimes we need to change our environment, including our workplace or relationships, or address circumstances that make it harder to feel happy and calm.

WHAT YOU WON'T FIND IN THIS BOOK

This is not a book on positive thinking.

While I've drawn from some techniques and authors who fall within the positive thinking movement, for me thinking positively isn't always the healthier choice. When someone tells me to ignore my concerns or assume the best will happen, that tends to ratchet up my anxiety because I start explaining why things are really as bad as I fear they are. At the same time I feel guilty about not being able to simply stop repeating my anxious thoughts.

In addition, being relentlessly positive can have downsides in daily life for anyone.

To borrow an example from author Barbara Ehrenreich in *Bright-sided: How Positive Thinking Is Undermining America*, when we drive it's safer to anticipate potential problems. Someone may cut us off in traffic, the driver approaching the intersection may be texting and not see the light turned red, and snow and ice may cause our car to skid whether we "think positive" or not. Assuming everything will always go well ironically would make us less apt to be prepared to avoid a crash.

Instead, the approaches I'm sharing will, I hope, help you address real concerns you have, enjoy what's good in your life, and create more of it.

The idea is to use our creativity to redirect our busy brains – which otherwise can work overtime at spiraling us into greater and greater anxiety –toward finding ways around obstacles, figuring out solutions, and becoming calmer and happier.

BEFORE YOU READ ON

The techniques and suggestions in this book are based on my personal experience. I've read widely on happiness, stress, and anxiety, gone to therapy, worked with a coach, experimented with different exercises, and attended workshops. Drawing from all of that I found what works for me. But I'm not a therapist, a mental health professional, or a doctor.

More important, I'm not you.

While I hope what I'm sharing will help, what makes me feel calmer or happier may not be best for you. Whatever you decide to try from this book, pay attention to the effect on you. Expand on what works. Set aside what doesn't. Or modify it to suit yourself.

Also, as with any new physical exercise, please talk with your doctor and/or mental health professional before you try anything new. Also, your healthcare provider may have treatment options to directly address anxiety that you might wish to try.

Speaking of health professionals, it's easy to assume that stress or anxiety is causing certain types of symptoms (such as stomach issues, sweating, muscle tension, dizziness, and many others). But that's not always the case even if you are going through a time when you're worried, grieving, or feeling heavily stressed.

In the months after my parents died (my parents were hit by a drunk driver in 2007) I experienced serious and significant emotional upset, depression, and stress. I had trouble sleeping for many months. I assumed that lack of sleep, grief, and the stress of making decisions for my dad's treatment were why I felt so tired. It took a tremendous effort simply to put one foot in front of the other to walk to work.

When I went to the doctor for an earache, though, I discovered that I had become anemic. After starting an iron supplement I was amazed how much more energy I had and how much better I felt.

I still had a lot of grieving to do, but improving my physical health made that and the rest of life less difficult.

GETTING THE MOST OUT OF THIS BOOK

To try to help as many readers as possible, this book includes numerous suggestions for easing anxiety. You don't need to try every one. Feel free to skim exercises, sections, or chapters if you start feeling overwhelmed. It's also fine to skip straight to the parts of the book that speak to your particular concerns. (I did my best to include descriptive chapter names and headings to help you identify those sections.)

You can always return later to see what you missed.

Finally, for those exercises you want to try, writing your responses rather than merely thinking about them will likely make the exercises more effective.

Part One

STUCK IN THE GROOVE

Chapter One

THE ANXIETY GROOVE

Once you know the emotional building blocks of anxiety, you can influence them.

- Chip Conley

*A*bout a year after I moved home from California, I got a full time job as a paralegal. I actually had a secretary I shared with the attorneys, and there was no computer in my office. So I didn't need to worry about work making my hands worse.

That didn't end my anxiety, though.

It came back multiple times in multiple guises. Usually it centered on work, such as when a new boss mandated that all paralegals have computers and do more of their own typing. (It was the 90s and not all employees had computers yet.) Other times it was more directly around health, such as when I played basketball on a hot day and inadvertently set off my tendinitis again. (To make it scarier, I worked at a small firm, and carpal tunnel and tendinitis were excluded from my health insurance.)

It seeped into other areas of my life, too, including relationships. As sympathetic as other people are, there's a limit to how often they want to hear the same fears repeated over and again or to hang out with someone whose conversation is an endless lament of what might go wrong.

Through it all I kept trying to think my way out of my fears. But all that happened most of the time was that I felt worse. What I didn't understand is that I was ruminating, something many people gripped by anxiety or depression do.

THINKING TOO MUCH

Ruminating can mean thinking deep thoughts about philosophical issues. But in this context it means repeating thoughts about distress or concerns.

To me, rumination is the biggest difference between my default approach and that of people who don't struggle the same way with anxiety. Sure, they worry from time to time, but it's proportionate to the issue they're facing. They deal with a concern as best they can, then set it aside and enjoy other parts of life whether or not they've found an answer.

One of my brothers, for example, worked for the same company for over two decades. He'd never done a professional job interview, as he'd transitioned into his career from an entry level assembly-line job he'd gotten through a friend's recommendation. While he took technical courses over the years to train for his work, he didn't have a college degree. Times had changed, though, and many jobs he otherwise qualified for based on experience now required a degree. He also had a large family depending on him for financial support.

Despite all that, when the company division my brother worked for announced it was closing he didn't lie awake every night or spend all his waking moments worrying whether or how he'd find a new job.

It's not that he didn't feel concerned that he was losing his job. He did.

needle out of the groove. Once it's out, the record moves on. Then it's a good time to deal with the real concern you're facing.

In Part 2 of this book I'll describe specific approaches I've found especially useful in doing that.

Before that, though, let's talk about another way we as writers tend to wear down that groove. Specifically, by asking *What If* and other questions that increase our anxiety.

Chapter Two

WHAT IF: A GREAT QUESTION FOR FICTION WRITING AND CATASTROPHIZING

Our questions determine our thoughts.

- Anthony Robbins, *Awaken the Giant Within: How To Take Immediate Control Of Your Mental, Emotional, Physical & Financial Destiny*

Storytelling is about conflict. As in, what if the worst possible thing happened next to your fictional character?

Or what if your potential reader feels stymied in her career, is struggling through a divorce, or fears never finding happiness?

Non-fiction writers, as the above paragraph shows, also deal in conflict in the form of problems. In fact, we look for problems. This book, for instance, tries to help writers solve the problems of too much anxiety and too little happiness.

WHAT IF?

All these conflicts start with two words, which are a key component of the exercises in my book Super Simple Story Structure (and in scores of books on writing and plotting):

- *What If?*
- *What if aliens landed and tried to take over the planet? (War Of The Worlds)*
- *What if just as they are about to move in together, a woman finds her boyfriend dead in his apartment? (My first Q.C. Davis novel, The Worried Man)*
- *What if a young woman struggling to finish a college degree discover she's pregnant despite that it's impossible? (My Awakening supernatural thriller series)*
- *What if you're diagnosed with breast cancer? What if you can't lose weight? What if your marriage fails? (any number of non-fiction books)*

All of these questions may be great prompts for books, but thinking this way is not healthy for life.

Yet these types of questions are key to keeping our fiction strong and our non-fiction ideas flowing because stories need conflict. The more intense or the larger the conflict, generally the more compelling the story.

For that reason, fiction writers spend a lot of time imagining the worst thing that could happen to our characters. If they get through that, we hand them another worst outcome, and another, and another.

Yes, they may prevail in the end (or not, depending on what type of writing you do), or your non-fiction book may offer solutions, but the worst possible things keep happening and happening and happening.

While in theory writers know the difference between imagining terrible things that could happen and those that are likely to occur, in practice it's often hard to turn off the *What Ifs* and worst-case scenario thinking.

In short, *What ifs* are great questions for prompting unhappiness and anxiety.

It's a big part of why, in my view, writers are particularly prone to anxiety, or maybe why anxious people are more apt to become writers, depending on whether you favor chickens or eggs.

IMAGINING CATASTROPHES

This type of thinking has a name. It's called catastrophizing.

It's how we get from *My boss sounded cranky when I spoke to her today* to *Tomorrow I'll be the one who's laid off* and *What if I can't pay my bills?* to *I probably won't find another job* and *I'll be a bag lady out on the street.*

This chain of thoughts may sound funny or exaggerated, but I experienced exactly that thought process for years after my move home from California. While the fears quieted over time, they continued to drive me long after it was clear that none of those things had happened or were likely to happen.

As a lawyer both at a large firm and on my own, I constantly took on so much work that I felt angry and tired much of the time. When running my own firm, I searched for new clients when I already felt stretched to the limit with the cases I had. Despite that I was not only paying my bills but had put away significantly for retirement I still operated out of fear.

That same anxiety kept me from hiring employees to help handle all that work or at least refraining from taking on more clients so that I could have a happier, healthier life.

I magnified my fears by asking myself questions like:

- *What if all my cases become dormant at once and I have nothing to do?*
- *What if six months down the road I've gotten successful outcomes for my clients and they don't need me anymore?*
- *What if I hire someone and a year from now I have to let that person go because there's not enough work?*

If you're feeling anxious, discouraged, or stuck in a dark mood, you too may be asking questions that lend themselves to answers that increase your unhappiness and stress. Even if you're feeling great, odds are choosing different questions can further enhance your sense of peace and happiness.

How do you do that? That's what we'll talk about in Chapters 7 and 8.

First, though, a few questions for you, and then a little about the past, the future, and perfectionism:

*A*re there *What Ifs* you return to again and again? If so, list a few of them.

_____
_____
_____
_____
_____

*H*ow do you feel when you ask yourself each *What If?*

_____
_____
_____
_____
_____

*M*ight you feel happier and calmer if you could stop?
_____

. . .

*A*re you afraid if you let go of your *What Ifs* you might overlook something important? _____

*A*re you willing to explore a different way of addressing your concerns? _____

Chapter Three

FORESHADOWING AND THE FEARS OF FUTURE PAST

I've lived through some terrible things in my life, some of which actually happened.

- Mark Twain

*A*t its heart, anxiety is about the past and the future, not whatever is happening right now.

We fear something — or many things — that might happen. Our hearts pound and our stomachs churn as we imagine every possible negative scenario, each one worse than the last. These are things we fear happening in the next day or year or decade.

We also often struggle to push against or change something that's already happened. We ask ourselves over and over why it happened or what we could have done differently. We look for someone or something to blame and feel angry, hurt, or sad not just once but many times over.

Often what we remember or fear is not an actual event but how we imagine things might change for the worse or what we imagine might never change for the better.

As writers, we're really good at this.

We can imagine all sorts of cause and effect chains. We can

attribute bad intentions or missteps to ourselves, to others, or to nature itself for that matter. The sky truly is the limit for what we can live and relive in our hearts and minds.

This may very well feel natural and right. After all, it's our job as writers to look under every rock for danger, conflict, and the causes of both.

Sometimes I think this is why storytellers have always been valued (if not well paid). Telling stories of dangers helps others avoid them or at least better cope with them. It offers, too, the solace that others have faced these things. That we are not alone in a frightening or sometimes-dark world.

So novelists foreshadow conflicts to come. Non-fiction writers hint at concerns raised or resolved later in the narrative. The old saying nearly always applies — if there's a gun on the table in Act 1, it needs to be used by the end of the book.

All good for writing. Not always so good for a happy, calm life in today's world.

It's another way that our writing can trip us up in our personal lives.

THE VALUE OF LOOKING FOR DANGER

Almost all people, not just writers, are wired to look for danger and remember it. That way we can avoid it in the future and survive. Further, every book I've read, and professional speaker I've heard, that addressed the subject of anxiety and panic attacks talks about the surge of adrenalin that relates to the fight-or-flight response. Our ancestors relied on that surge.

Those ancestors most likely to survive and pass on their genes weren't the ones who took a deep breath, became calm, and rationally thought through what the charging tiger meant. They also weren't the ones who sat breathing rhythmically on a rock, letting go of the outside world.

They were the ones who, in an instant and spurred by that

adrenalin, fled or fought and lived to tell the tale.

Today, though, that adrenalin surge sometimes makes it harder to face the day-to-day stresses that wear on us and wake us at night.

PAST AND FUTURE

To complicate our quest for calm, being aware of and alert to danger has significant advantages in modern life.

Imagining that your supervisor's frown may be about the email you sent a moment ago might cue you that there's an issue with your job performance. This is especially true if your supervisor often fails to tell employees when she's unhappy with them until it's too late to fix whatever's wrong.

Similarly, noticing your partner's or friend's snarky comment can cause you to spot a problem in your relationship before it grows.

The ability to analyze the past, search for causes of problems, and draw lessons from them also can be key to doing well in life. Vividly remembering how sick you got after eating meat left out on the counter to thaw reminds you to keep it in the refrigerator next time.

So there are good reasons to spend some mental energy figuring out if your supervisor's frown last Friday meant she was unhappy with your work.

On the other hand, your supervisor may have been thinking about her weekend plans having been cancelled, not about you. And if you've done well at your job month after month or year after year, constant vigilance, rather than improving your life, may be exhausting you.

In addition, if we ruminate about things in the past that we can't change we do more than increase our feelings of anxiety. We often feel hopeless and helpless because there is literally nothing we can do to change what already occurred.

Luckily, our imagination and our ability to see around life's corners or into the past can also be used to become happier and more peaceful, as we'll talk about in Part 2.

First, though, a word about the role perfectionism and control can play in anxiety (after a few questions).

*A*re there things that happened already that you go over again and again in your mind? _____

*I*f so, what are they?

_____

_____

_____

_____

*A*fter each one, note whether reimagining those scenes has helped you change your future actions.

*W*hat recurring concerns do you have about the future? (Write them down and set them aside for Chapter 8.)

_____

_____

_____

_____

_____

_____

_____

Chapter Four

PERFECTLY ANXIOUS AND IN CONTROL

I've yet to meet an absolute perfectionist whose life was filled
with inner peace.

-- Richard Carlson, *Don't Sweat The Small Stuff...And It's All
Small Stuff: Simple Ways To Keep The Little Things From Taking Over
Your Life*

For many people anxiety relates to the desire for
perfection. This belief that we can and should be
perfect can pose a particular hazard for writers and other creative
people because we have good imaginations that are always
engaged. Our busy minds can always imagine how much better,
or how perfect, almost anything could be just as we can imagine
everything that could possibly go wrong.

Because it's almost impossible to do anything perfectly,
though, or to have a perfect outcome, the desire for perfection
almost by definition creates anxiety.

This may be why the things I stress over also are the ones that
I feel fairly certain I'm good at.

I'm confident, for example, that I'm good at legal analysis and
writing. It's beyond a feeling. I've won appeals that depended on

those skills, and the appellate court adopted my line of reasoning and sometimes my words. Also, other attorneys whose abilities I admire have turned to me for aid in this area.

While when I'm nearly finished with a novel I often feel doubts, overall I feel pretty good about my fiction writing. I've seen enough reviews, good and bad, to feel I've assessed my skills fairly accurately.

So why the anxiety?

Because I'm not measuring myself against what someone similar to me would do most of the time. I'm measuring myself against what the perfect attorney/writer/sister/friend/partner would do every single moment of every single day forever.

There's also a control issue going on.

Some of us who feel anxiety also occasionally take our fears of the future a step further. We begin to believe that worry in itself can somehow stave off bad things.

My mom (the person I basically learned how to worry from) said something telling as we waited together at a hospital when my dad needed heart surgery. She said it happened because she hadn't worried about his heart, only his back. (He had a history of serious back issues.) It had never occurred to her to be concerned about his heart because he'd always been in overall good health, exercised, and didn't smoke.

This idea that you can control the world by worrying is, for a lot of us, yet another reason it's so hard to let go of anxiety. On some level, we believe we need it.

Someone I knew early in my career as a lawyer reinforced all my fears about letting go of worry. (Yes, I have fears about not having enough fear.)

The firm where I worked evaluated us by how many of the hours we worked per year could be billed to clients. At her first three six-month reviews in a row a lawyer I'll call Susan was told that she needed to bill more hours.

At each review she claimed the low billable hours weren't her fault. She wasn't getting enough quality work. (She'd been offered work she thought was beneath her and turned it down.) Also, the firm itself was slow, though other attorneys were meeting their hours requirements. She left each review with no concern — no worry — about finding or doing more work.

She was the only one surprised when the firm let her go.

Part of me envies her. Because sometimes it seems I'm always second-guessing myself.

Did I work hard enough? Did I clearly communicate?

Did I say something that upset someone? Am I a good enough friend, boss, employee, lawyer, writer, teacher? Is there more I ought to or could be doing to improve?

It's tiring. I'd like to take a rest, be that person who throws up her hands and says there's nothing I can do and clearly any problem I have is someone else's fault.

Yet that person really, really scares me. Because she did get fired.

After about six months she landed on her feet, but rather than making her own choice about her career she let others make the decision for her.

LETTING GO – YAY OR NAY?

Recognizing that perfectionism and the desire for control can increase anxiety and make life harder doesn't make it easy to let go of either. It's not like you can simply say to yourself, "Let go" and it happens.

I've tried.

Part of the challenge is I'm not convinced letting go is a good idea. I don't want to be Susan, that lawyer who got fired. She had no fear. She had no desire to be perfect. And she lost her job.

My default is to say that if she had been a worrier, if she had striven for perfection, that combined fear and desire might have pushed her to do something about her situation.

And sometimes anxiety does motivate us. But the cost is high. For a long time I felt I couldn't rest. No matter what I did, it was never enough. I could always imagine something more I could have done. Some slightly better — or perfect — outcome.

While it might have helped spur me to action, the chronic worry made it harder to get things done. I managed, but it took a lot of effort to do a good job while at the same time spinning through the fears in my head.

In fact, you can be more aware of what's really happening when you're not wracked by fear. You can also better position yourself in life when you're not draining your energy through fearful and repetitive thoughts.

So how do we know it's safe to let go?

The key is to recognize three things.

First, that we'll do a better job at whatever we're doing if we relax enough to concentrate rather than running stressed and anxious thoughts through our minds.

Second, that there's a difference between worry and concern.

Susan's problem wasn't that she didn't worry. She didn't need debilitating, heart-pounding, wake-you-in-the-middle-of-the-night fear to make her aware of the issue. Her supervisors flagged the problem more than once.

She chose, however, to ignore the situation rather than take responsibility for what she could do to address it.

I'm not someone who tends toward irresponsibility. If you're reading this I'm guessing you also don't. Perfectionists and anxious people are often ones who feel overly responsible. We check every detail and every box. We check other people's work, too.

So, faced with that same situation, not only would I not have needed worry, I wouldn't have needed the supervisor. Because it mattered to me to do a good job, I would have already paid attention to how many hours I billed and, if I wasn't meeting my billing targets for more than a week or two, set to work finding a solution. (And, in fact, throughout my career at that firm I did just that.)

My concern about doing a good job made worrying unnecessary.

Third, if something's out of our control, worrying will not magically give us power over the situation. It will only make it harder to deal with.

The Susan example is one that was largely within her control, so it's a little easier to say that concern about it would remedy the problem.

In contrast, my parents being hit by a drunk driver was entirely out of my control.

Worrying about my dad's treatment (he lived a little over six weeks after the crash and had two emergency surgeries) or the criminal prosecution against the driver didn't give me any control over either. It actually made it harder to do what I needed to do to stay informed and make decisions, taking us back to the first point. Worrying makes it harder to do what we need to do, not easier.

So let's say you're convinced it is okay to let go of anxiety. You still need to know how to do it.

Which is what the rest of this book is about.

Part Two

REWRITING OUR INNER LIVES

Chapter Five

GETTING OUT OF THE GROOVE

A low mood is not the time to analyze your life. To do so is emotional suicide.

-- Richard Carlson, *Don't Sweat The Small Stuff...And It's All Small Stuff: Simple Ways To Keep The Little Things From Taking Over Your Life*

*A*s the quote above suggests, it's hard to figure out how to increase our happiness in the midst of anxiety or a depressed mood. It's also hard to let go of anxious thoughts or replace them with more calming ones with your heart racing and gut clenching.

That's why before I cover choosing and revising your words and actions and other techniques, I want to talk about ways to bounce your needle out of the anxiety groove.

I call these pattern interrupts because they're quick strategies for breaking the cycle of anxiety. The ones that work for me may help you and/or you may figure out your own based on what I've suggested. Either way, having strategies ready before you awake in the middle of the night with your heart pounding or before panic overtakes you makes it easier to shift your emotional state.

It also should ease your mind about your ability to handle anxiety in the future.

Here's the short list of the pattern interrupts I've found most helpful. Then I'll talk a little more about each one.

- Quick Catchphrases
- Movement/exercise
- Singing
- Entertainment
- Audio

QUICK CATCHPHRASES

Catchphrases are short phrases you can easily remember and repeat. You'll use them to replace or stave off anxious thoughts. The key is to write the phrase or phrases in advance so in the moment no thought is required. I think of them almost like magic words to send my anxiety into the ether. Or at least dampen it.

You can also write a phrase that reinforces something positive you want to remember about a situation or yourself.

During the years I worked as a paralegal, I felt concerned — okay, I worried, sometimes obsessively — about being laid off. I felt well-qualified on paper to seek another paralegal job. But with the world moving more and more toward computers and keyboarding, I feared not being able to find another job that wouldn't require me to type a lot.

The second part of that fear was not unrealistic. Most paralegal jobs that I'd seen advertised included secretarial work or a lot of data entry.

The first part was unlikely, as at the time I was most plagued by worry the firm was doing well. The clients liked me, and the lawyers I worked for were happy with my work and kept giving me more advanced projects.

Yet my fears persisted, often in the form of *What Ifs*. (*What if I lose this job and never find another?*)

That's when I first came up with a catchphrase. With it, I reminded myself that I had gotten through tough times and challenges before. So I told myself:

I'm like a cat, I always land on my feet.

That quick and slightly silly phrase captured in an instant how I'd gone from no easily-defined skills that didn't require typing to finishing a graduate paralegal program and finding a job I loved that didn't reinjure my hands and arms. While I still didn't know how I would deal with it if I lost that job, the phrase reminded me that it would almost certainly be easier than what I'd already gone through to get it.

These days when anxiety troubles me it's often because whatever I'm doing at the moment isn't paying off. That could be trying a new advertising platform for my novels or dealing with someone difficult in connection with a legal project or a class I teach. To cut off my fears that I'll never make things work, or there's no way to improve how things are right now, I'll think:

There's more than one way to skin a cat.

This phrase creates a somewhat gruesome picture, and that's part of the point. It derails whatever anxious thoughts I'm running over and over in my brain. It also reminds me that if what I'm doing isn't working, there's something else I can try.

Catchphrases are particularly good for those middle-of-the-night panicked feelings.

I don't know about you, but the middle of the night and first thing in the morning are the times anxiety is most likely to hit. With nothing to do but lie there and think, my worries multiply and feel more and more real. Maybe it's because day-to-day concerns aren't occupying my brain. Faced with a vacuum, my mind fills it with worries.

A catchphrase can be a great way to derail that anxiety train.

Prepare it in advance so no problem solving or analytic skills are required when you're feeling anxious. And keep it simple. Your goal, especially in the middle of the night, is to relax and rest, not start your brain working on anything new. (I'll talk in Chapter 8 about ways to engage your mind to address your concerns more actively.)

Once you have your phrase, use it to interrupt your spinning thoughts. Every time your brain shifts to another anxious thought, you respond with the same phrase.

I repeat mine like a broken record until I feel calmer and the anxious thoughts become less intense.

PHYSICAL MOVEMENT AND EXERCISE

If you're fortunate enough to have use of your physical body, movement and exercise also can be great pattern interrupts.

Exercise of any sort pulls us out of our minds at least temporarily. It also sends endorphins through us, helping raise our mood.

The exercise doesn't need to be physically demanding to change our moods.

I was in a cast from my toes to my right knee for over ten weeks this year. When I felt anxious, I often grabbed my crutches and did some of the knee bending exercises my doctor had prescribed for me. Focusing on keeping my balance on my one good foot required all my attention and interrupted my thoughts.

When I finished I returned to sitting and pinwheeled my arms. I'm sure I looked a little silly sitting on the couch and rotating my arms, but the very silliness of it helped shift my thoughts.

Now that I'm on two feet I often do the hopping exercises my physical therapist taught me to rehab my healing foot. It gets my blood pumping and burns off some excess nervous energy. Jumping jacks also work for this. Often after I've done ten I'm able to calm my thoughts at least a little bit.

Walking, though, is ideal. In addition to the pluses of exercise, it gets me outside, which often lifts my mood in itself. And there's an added boost for writers. According to a Stanford University study walking boosts your creativity by 60%.

Exercising can be especially vital for writers.

Writing often involves a lot of sitting. If you write full-time, you may spend anywhere from three to ten hours a day (or more) writing. If you already work in an office during the day and you come home and write for an hour every night at a desk or table, you're adding 10% or more to your sitting (or standing still) time.

For that reason, I set a timer for 30-40 minutes when I write. When it goes off, I spend five minutes doing simple exercises. Stretching to balance off my keyboard position, going up and down flights of stairs, lifting a five-pound weight. It helps derail anxious thoughts and improves my mood overall.

Using a timer offers another bonus.

It segregates that 30-40 minutes and makes it less likely I'll become distracted. If an email notification dings, I tell myself I'll check when the timer goes off. Similarly, if it crosses my mind to check something on social media, I push that idea aside until my writing time is done.

SINGING

Sometimes you're not physically able to get up and move around. Or it's the middle of the night and you're not about to hop around in the dark. (And if you did, it'd probably make it too hard to get back to sleep.)

You can use catchphrases at those moments. But maybe the phrase isn't quite getting you out of that thought pattern.

At those moments, I find singing a line or two aloud or in my head is great for derailing anxious or discouraged thoughts. It almost forces my brain to focus on the song rather than worry.

I've found the best songs are happy, fun, or silly ones.

When I was having a lot of trouble sleeping in my cast I often sang a verse and chorus from *My Favorite Things* from *The Sound Of Music*.

It has an upbeat tune. Also, the lyrics are fitting, as they're about things that the songwriter loves and uses to get past fear. Finally, it's hard to run through nightmare scenarios about ill health or financial ruin while simultaneously singing to myself about warm mittens, roses, and kittens.

Another favorite of mine is *Keep On The Sunny Side*, an old Carter Family tune. Its theme is pretty much what it sounds like. (You can watch a YouTube video of me singing and playing it at https://youtu.be/LIwiL_R4AfA.)

Sometimes I just hum part of the old Simon and Garfunkel *The 59th Street Bridge Song (Feelin' Groovy)* with "feelin' groovy" being the only words of it that I know. It works because the word groovy sounds a lot like goofy. And it is a sort of goofy word that isn't used much anymore. It helps cut off my more serious thoughts.

I sing in my head during the day as well if anxious thoughts are popping into my mind repeatedly or my body is tensing. It's one of the best ways I've found to quickly shift my mood.

BOOKS, VIDEOS, MOVIES, GAMES, AND OTHER ENTERTAINMENT

For some people reading a book, playing a game (video, board game, or other) or watching a movie or video can interrupt anxious or discouraging thoughts.

I've listed these toward the end, though, for two reasons. First, you can't always take a break to do one of these things. It's easier to say a phrase or sing a line of a song in your head or even squeeze in a quick stretch or hop without interrupting your whole day.

Second, some of these activities are passive and allow your mind to wander. Much as I love to read, unless a book grabs me from the first word I can simply keep spinning my worry-based thoughts in the back of my mind as I read. The same is true for watching a movie or television series.

But there are exceptions, and you may find ones that work very well for you.

When I was in the cast and feeling very anxious, I watched The Lizzie Bennet Diaries. I'd heard about the series but hadn't checked it out before. It's a modern-day retelling of *Pride and Prejudice*, my favorite book, through a vlog. The videos are usually 2-6 minutes long.

The new take on the story and characters and the different from of storytelling fascinated me. Whenever I watched, all other thoughts flew out of my head, including my worries.

So if playing a videogame or engaging with a particular type of story draws you in and fully occupies your mind, that may work as a pattern interrupt for you.

AUDIO

I've given Audio its own category because it played a key role in managing my fears and my physical discomfort this year and helping me sleep.

If you've ever slept with a cast, you know it feels like your limb is lying on a thin layer of cloth over solid concrete. Not a great sleeping posture whether you tend toward anxiety or not. Also, while the pain wasn't intense, no matter how I positioned myself eventually my foot would hurt and I'd need to rearrange.

Anxious feelings about whether the cast had been put on too tight for my circulation or I'd reinjured my foot (I fell on it a couple times) added to my difficulty sleeping. And the less I slept at night the more anxious I felt during the day.

So I put my Audible app on a sleep timer and played *Pride and Prejudice* as I lay down to sleep. I chose it for three reasons.

First, I've read it so often I know it backwards and forwards. I didn't feel the need to remain awake to hear what happened.

Second, while the story has plenty of conflict, there are no viscerally disturbing images or plot turns the way there are in thrillers and horror. And third, I downloaded the edition read by Shiromi Arserio, the narrator who produced three of my own books and whose voice I love. She is one of those people who could read the proverbial phone book and make it sound compelling.

All these things combined made it the perfect way to occupy enough of my brain to shut out my fears but not too much of it so as to keep me awake.

When I woke in the middle of the night I often put the audio on again to help me transition back to sleep. I probably listened to the book three times through over the summer.

You may find a book or podcast that does the same for you. Look for one that won't heighten anxious or excited feelings. (So probably no politics, unless you truly find that soothing.)

Overall, having a handful of techniques for bouncing yourself out of the anxiety groove will help you calm yourself and make it easier to apply the techniques in the rest of this book.

Experiment to see what's good for you.

The pattern interrupt that works in one situation may not in another, and what's most effective may change with different life situations. But I hope you'll end with one or more techniques that help you.

*A*re there shows, games, or books that absorb you so completely that you forget everything else? If so, list three of them.

_____

_____

_____

. . .

*W*hat are some catchphrases you can say to block out or override the anxious or discouraging thoughts?

_____

_____

_____

_____

*D*o the phrases you wrote reflect your strengths or remind you that you can handle challenges? _____

*I*f not, can you rewrite them or come up with new ones that do?

_____

_____

_____

_____

*L*ist three songs that make you feel happy when you hear them.

_____

_____

_____

*W*rite out a line or two of each song that's catchy enough that you could replay it in your mind in the middle of the night (or sing it).

_____

_____

_____

*W*hich of the other pattern interrupts seems like it would work best for you?

_____

_____

*W*hat are some other pattern interrupts you could use? List five even if they seem a little out there.

_____

_____

_____

_____

Chapter Six

PERSPECTIVE AND TIME TRAVEL

Ask yourself the question, "Will this matter a year from now?"
-- Richard Carlson, *Don't Sweat The Small Stuff...And It's All Small Stuff: Simple Ways To Keep The Little Things From Taking Over Your Life*

*a*nother way to use your imagination to bounce you out of the anxiety groove, or when you face challenges that seem overwhelming, is to engage in some mental time travel.

There will be times when something truly devastating happens. Something that won't seem like an inconvenience or irritation whether you view it from the lens of a year ago, a year from now, or ten years from now. But for most things imagining yourself a year away from whatever it is will help you put it into perspective.

To try this out:

*T*hink of a situation you are feeling anxious or unhappy about and imagine that you are one year down the road.

. . .

*H*ow do you feel about the situation as you look back on it?

_____
_____
_____

*H*ow did it resolve?

_____
_____
_____

*D*oes life seem more manageable now that you're a year beyond it?_____

*D*oes it seem as horrible or frightening as it did a year ago?_____

*I*f it still looks like a disaster from this perspective do you see some ways that you helped yourself cope with it? _____

*N*ow imagine it is one year ago and you know that this event is coming:

. . .

*H*ow do you view it as you look ahead to it happening?

_____
_____
_____

*D*o you have ideas about how to manage it? _____

*D*oes it seem like the end of the world or more like something challenging that you will need to deal with?

_____

*I*f it's too hard to picture of yourself a year ago or a year in the future, create a character in your mind facing a similar issue and imagine that character dealing with it.

_____
_____
_____
_____

*W*hether it's you or the character write in detail how it feels to be on the other side of the challenge.

_____
_____
_____
_____

. . .

*W*rite about what you or your character did to get to that point.

_____

_____

_____

_____

*N*ow that you've read a couple ideas about helping yourself feel at least somewhat less anxious, let's talk about specific techniques to both address problems and increase calm and happiness.

We'll start with the questions you ask yourself.

Chapter Seven

BETTER WHAT IFS AND OTHER QUESTIONS

Learning to ask empowering questions in moments of crisis...pulled me through some of the roughest times in my life.

- Anthony Robbins in *Awaken the Giant Within: How To Take Immediate Control Of Your Mental, Emotional, Physical & Financial Destiny*

Those of us who tend toward anxiety or unhappiness typically spin the same issues and concerns over and over in our minds. Often that happens in the form of questions, such as *What if I never get another job? What if my daughter always hates me?*

Rewriting the questions we ask or deliberately writing more helpful ones puts all that energy and effort to work for you. Rather than your questions intensifying your anxiety, they can generate solutions, excitement, happiness, positive actions, and calm.

POST-CALIFORNIA

I first discovered the power of questions during the year of intense anxiety after I moved home from California. A friend, seeing me struggle with fears about my repetitive stress injury and how it could affect my job prospects, recommended *Awaken The Giant Within* by Anthony Robbins.

Robbins' theory is that all of us (anxious or not) think through asking ourselves questions.

If we ask questions that are more likely to lead to empowering answers we can become happier and more successful. If we ask disempowering questions, we add to our anxiety and stress, making it harder to deal with life's challenges. Those questions also make it harder to enjoy and appreciate what's already great in our lives.

This is true whether we're facing a small challenge or one that's life-threatening.

Let's start with a life-threatening one.

THE MAN WHO WAS RUN OVER

An attorney I know was run over by a car while he was mowing his lawn. One moment he was fine and happy and enjoying a beautiful day. The next he was in an ambulance with multiple severe leg fractures and glass in his eyes.

After surgery to remove the glass, another surgeon came to see him with bad news. He would need multiple surgeries on his leg to try to save it. At best, he'd need hardware put in that would later be removed. At worst he'd lose his leg.

Being human, his first question was *Why me?*

The surgeon stopped him. He said that it happened and there was nothing to be gained by asking why. Instead, the question was what were they going to do about it.

Some people might be upset by the doctor's blunt bedside

manner and see it as unsympathetic. But my friend said that it worked for him. He decided in that instant that the surgeon was right. He never asked himself again why this had happened to him. Instead, at each surgery and each stage of rehab he said "What's the next step?" and "What can I do to get the best outcome?" (More on that and the rest of his story in Chapter 20.)

FEAR SPIRALS

The surgeon likely would agree with Anthony Robbins, who points out that if we ask ourselves negative questions we will get negative answers. That makes sense to me because human brains look for cause and effect. If you ask your brain why bad things happen to you, it'll start looking for answers. Those answers are more apt to reflect your fears than any objective truth, though they will feel quite real.

A few you might be familiar with (as I am):

- You always have bad luck
- You did something wrong to deserve punishment
- You are prone to making mistakes
- You are always in the wrong place at the wrong time

None of these answers is likely to help you feel better, handle whatever you're facing, or improve your life.

Questions also can lead to a spiral of fear. Here's a typical thought pattern for me:

- *I have a sharp pain in my side.*
- *What if it's appendicitis?*
- *It's probably not, and I don't want to go to the emergency room, but what if I wait too long and my appendix bursts?*
- *Still, what if my health insurance doesn't cover this hospital and I didn't really need to go and now I'll have this huge bill?*

- *If I do need surgery, what if there are complications and I don't survive?*
- *Or I'm in the hospital for months and can't get any work done?*

As you can see, my concerns nearly always center around health and money. You can substitute your own particular worries above, but you get the idea.

NEW QUESTIONS TO DEAL WITH PROBLEMS

By rewriting your questions, you can make it more likely you will do something different in the future. Also that you'll improve your mood and life right now.

This technique helped me when the worry was something totally out of my control. Also when something I did contributed to a challenge I faced.

For instance, let's say you got fired and it was partly because you arrived at work late every day. The questions and answers above about why bad things happen wouldn't motivate you to get to work on time in the future and possibly do better at your next job.

To the contrary, the answers assume there's something wrong with you at your core, something that can't be changed, or that the world is simply against you. So all you have to look forward to is more bad things.

Suppose rather than *Why do bad things happen to me?* you wrote a new question: *How can I be a more valuable employee at my next job?*

That question is empowering because it contains the assumption that there is, in fact, something you can do, and it prompts your brain to provide an answer.

One response might be that you could be on time each day. More than that, though, this question might prompt answers about developing new technical skills, learning how to better get along with people, or finding a job that is a better fit so that you want to get there early each day.

It also suggests other great questions, such as the one about how you can get a job that's a better fit. Or what about: *How can I get a job I absolutely love?*

To rewrite my questions and thought chain from above that centered on fears about pain, I can start simply:

- *I have a sharp pain in my side.*
- *What's the best first step to take to see if this is something serious?*

That question can prompt me to take practical actions rather than obsessing over my fear.

I might also ask things like:

Is there something relatively benign that this could be?

If I were advising a friend, at what point would I suggest going to the emergency room?

What can I do to feel safe if I want to wait a little while and see if I feel better?

The first question reminds me that there are lots of less serious problems this pain could indicate.

The second question, about what I'd suggest to a friend, allows me to decide on a course of action a little more objectively. I may still feel anxious, but by imagining a friend asking advice I can set that aside and balance the competing concerns of health and well-being versus the expense, hassle, and risks of an emergency room visit.

The last question reassures me that I'm not putting myself in peril by not going to the emergency room immediately. I might answer that I should keep my cell phone near me or call a friend who will call me back and check on me in ten or fifteen minutes to make sure I'm okay.

For all our questions and answers, imagination provides a huge benefit. It can help us think of actions and choose words that make us feel calmer and make it more likely we'll do what's best for ourselves rather than get mired in fear and unhappiness.

I think of it as making my overactive brain work for me rather than against me.

As I'll talk about more in the next chapter, questions can also be used proactively. Let's say three of my coworkers are laid off this week, and there are rumors of more cutbacks to come.

Here are some questions I can ask myself as soon as my stomach starts tightening (or before):

- *What can I do today that makes it less likely I'll be next to be laid off?*
- *How can I find out how I am doing at work?*
- *Who do I trust who could help me improve my work performance?*
- *What can I do to position myself better in the job market?*
- *What other employers would I enjoy working for?*

All of these questions are designed to focus on solutions rather than problems. They are far less likely to spark anxious feelings than most questions I'd normally ask myself in that situation.

Whether he was conscious of it or not, these are probably the kinds of questions my brother asked himself when his company announced his division would shut down. Rather than imagining all the terrible things that might happen when he lost his job, he shifted quickly to doing things that would help him find a new one.

Choosing what questions to ask can be helpful even in truly tragic situations that you can do nothing to change.

My dad survived for about six and a half weeks after being hit by a drunk driver. He made it through two emergency surgeries, but in the end his injuries were too severe. My mom died at the scene. In the street. It would be hard to exaggerate how angry and distraught I felt during my dad's hospitalization and for the year afterwards.

But I tried to ask myself some empowering questions. Two I borrowed from Anthony Robbins' *Awaken The Giant Within*.

The first one can be a true challenge if you're facing real tragedy. The question is *What's great about this?*

With something like the death of a loved one that seems like a horrible question to ask. And I don't suggest asking at the moment it happens. But I did find an answer. Not about my parents' deaths, but about what happened after.

I thought about the off duty police detective who saw the crash, followed the driver (who fled the scene), and contacted local police. I thought about the police officers who ensured that the drunk driver was arrested and who came to court regularly to testify.

Also about a paramedic from my parents' parish. When transporting my dad a few weeks after the crash for a medical test she called his pastor on her phone for him, knowing it would make Dad feel a little better to hear the pastor's voice.

Then there was my cousin who came to the emergency room the night of the crash. (He'd been called because the woman who saw the crash knew my parents and my cousin.) He stayed with me until other members of my family got there. Friends helped me go through my parents' house to find documents we needed, picked up groceries for me, and called relatives to tell them about my dad's death.

So my answer to what was good was that there are so many helpful, kind people in the world who will go the extra mile to help others.

That answer didn't make my parents' deaths okay. I still felt awful much of the time.

But it did help me remember what was good in the world and in my life at a time when everything seemed dark. And about a year later when I started feeling much more like myself, I felt reassured at how many truly good people exist. That feeling has stayed with me, and now it's what I focus on far more often than the awful way my parents died.

I also asked another question Robbins suggests asking each day: *Who do I love and who loves me?*

That question reminded me how fortunate I was to have my friends and my family and made me think of the ways we support each other.

It also got me through my darkest moment.

I was trudging to work, struggling to summon the energy to put one foot in front of the other and ignore the feeling of dread as I anticipated the combative emails I knew would be waiting for me in a particularly difficult case. I saw a CTA bus. The thought crossed my mind that if I stepped in front of it, all this pain would be over.

Immediately, though, I flashed to how my brothers and nieces and nephews would feel if I did that.

That very day I put in for a leave at work. I'd chosen not to do that before because I thought I was better off working and staying occupied. I also knew it would hurt my chances of a promotion (which it did). But being in touch with my feelings about the people who love me in that brief frightening moment reset my priorities. It also made me realize that working sixty or seventy hours a week was not, for me, the way to deal with my grief.

I like to think I never would have harmed myself whether I asked those two questions each day or not. But I'm grateful that I did because that was the moment I started pulling out of the darkness.

In the next chapter we'll talk in more depth about questions and solutions to challenges you face. But first:

. . .

*W*hat is a challenge that you feel anxious or upset about and think about repeatedly?

_____

_____

*W*hat is one thing, however small, you could do today that might help you feel a little calmer about it?

_____

*L*ist 5 questions you could ask that are designed to see something good in the situation.

_____

_____

_____

_____

_____

*I*f you're stuck on what to ask yourself, what would you ask a friend you were trying to help sort through the same problem?

_____

_____

_____

_____

_____

Chapter Eight

USING QUESTIONS PROACTIVELY

*I*n the past when I felt anxious I looked around until I found what I thought was making me feel that way. I tried to think myself out of anxiety by asking these types of questions:

- *Why do I feel anxious?*
- *What's going wrong that's causing these feelings?*
- *What might happen today that I'm worried about?*

Because it's rare that life is perfect, there was always something that was a concern or might become one in the future. And sometimes significant things were happening that would cause anyone to feel anxious.

The problem with these questions is that if you ask them, consciously or unconsciously, you'll likely spiral into greater anxiety. Similarly, if you're apt to wake up feeling discouraged or in a depressed mood, these questions and their answers will likely sink you deeper into feelings of helplessness or hopelessness.

But what if instead you asked yourself:

- *What can I do this very moment to feel just a little calmer?*
- *What can I do this very moment to feel just a little happier?*

I included the phrases "this very moment" and "just a little" intentionally.

Those words stop my mind from pushing back and insisting that it's impossible to be calm or happy given what I'm facing. Even in awful moments, such as after my parents' deaths, I could almost always do something in the moment to feel just a little better.

BECOMING JUST A LITTLE CALMER

When something you fear looms or you feel anxious regardless what's happening around you try asking and answering those two questions.

To give an idea how this works I've listed common answers my mind gives me below.

- Drinking a glass of water (especially first thing in the morning when I'm apt to be dehydrated)
- Thinking of someone I care about and hoping that person will have a good day
- Stretching (hands, wrists, shoulders, feet, any part of my body)
- Reimagining a good moment from the day or week before
- Writing things I'm grateful for (more on that in Chapter 10)
- Reading a page of an encouraging book (more on that in Chapter 12)

Your answers will vary, I'm sure, from mine or from anyone else's. But however you answer, the two questions about feeling better are likely to provoke answers of things you can do quickly. If you do them, you'll likely feel a little calmer and happier than if you regularly ask and answer the first three questions in this chapter.

Sometimes you'll find there really was nothing of concern and things are going pretty well.

You may have awakened unsettled, but the feeling was a holdover from a bad dream, a result of the chemicals that shift your body to wakefulness from sleep, or an ingrained and unconscious habit of scanning for trouble the moment you awaken (or throughout the day).

Regardless, once you feel a little better you can check in with yourself. See if there is any concern you need to address. In fact, if you make a practice of checking in it'll reassure you that it's fine to first get a bit calmer and then take care of whatever needs taking care of.

Happily, you'll be more able to keep it in perspective and deal with it in a calmer frame of mind.

For example, let's say you have a presentation that afternoon and you don't feel fully prepared for it. Now that you've taken a few minutes to feel better you can decide when you can fit in preparing for that presentation. Even if you realize you have little time to prepare, you can ask yourself what's the quickest thing that you can do to do the best job possible under the circumstances.

Intense anxiety, though, may require more than shifting your mindset. I find that's particularly so if I'm trying to deal with a significant issue that sparks anxiety.

Because of that, this next technique uses questions more proactively to acknowledge fear and take action.

ACKNOWLEDGEMENT AND ACTION

In Chapter 5 I talked about a catchphrase I used to help deal with my fear about losing my paralegal job.

But I also used questions to help me take action to address that fear.

I started in a way that scared me: by acknowledging that the thing I feared could happen. I said to myself, *Okay, what if I do get laid off?*

Instead of imagining possible nightmare scenarios, though, I wrote a list of all the ways that I was now better qualified than I had been the first time around when looking for a paralegal job. It included things like owning business clothes to wear to inter-views, having a couple years experience, understanding how to draft my resume and what to highlight, having job references, and being much more practiced at interviewing.

I also reminded myself regularly of the good things that had come out of this change in my life. I had set out to find a job that would allow me to pay my bills. But I'd found work I really liked working with people I respected. Also, I was learning about a whole other industry and profession.

Then I asked a follow up question:

- *If I knew now that I'd be laid off in a year, what would be the very best way I could prepare for that?*

The year timeframe in the question gave me room to think more long-term about my career, rather than simply the survival aspect of keeping a job.

And the question addressed the kernel of truth in my fear. The world was becoming more computer-based, and most paralegals I knew did a lot of data entry. It would be a challenge to find another job in my field that didn't require typing. After making my list of advantages, I felt more confident I could do that if needed.

But why not explore what else I could do to have more options (whether or not the threat of layoffs loomed)?

To increase my non-database skills, I took a course in being an investigative paralegal. Over twenty years later some of what I learned now gives me a starting point for research and plot twists in my Q.C. Davis mystery/suspense series.

I also looked at graduate programs in English and Writing, which would build on my college major. I went so far as to apply to a couple to see whether I could do something else for a living if I ever needed to. I asked for informational interviews with people who did other kinds of jobs that I thought I might like.

The more I did, the better I felt. I shifted from feeling anxious to feeling excited about possibilities if I ever wanted or needed to find a different job or type of work.

A couple years later I was still a paralegal at the same firm. Because he saw how much I liked helping at trials and how much I'd advanced in my work, my boss suggested I might want to go to law school.

I'd never planned to become a lawyer. Oddly, law wasn't one of the options I'd looked at, maybe because the people I knew who were lawyers had been set on it since they were in grade school or high school. Because of all the thinking and exploring I'd done earlier, though, I now felt open to the idea. It set me off on a new career that was exciting, challenging, and financially rewarding in a way I'd never experienced before.

For decades since then I've drawn on everything I learned when I went through that exploration and information gathering phase. As an attorney, it helped me better understand my clients' businesses. As a writer, it gave me a much broader knowledge of career paths, jobs, and workplaces than I'd have if I could rely only on my own experience and that of people I know personally.

Taking action doesn't need to span months or years or require major changes in your life, though.

As another job example — can you tell how much of my anxiety focused on work? — during a particularly challenging few months for me as a lawyer I met with a recruiter.

She didn't have a current position to suggest. Recruiters usually are best at getting you the same kind of job you already have, which was exactly what I didn't want. But she did suggest ways to reframe my experience if I wanted to change to a different type of practice down the road.

I never did what she suggested. But I'm grateful to her for showing me that there might be a path I hadn't thought about before. It helped me let go of some of my anxiety about feeling stuck in the position I had.

In the next chapter we'll talk about another way to revise what you say to yourself. Before we do, though, try your hand at proactive questions.

*L*ist 5 things you could do in this moment to feel just a little calmer or happier.

_____

_____

_____

_____

_____

*I*s there a significant concern that sparks your anxiety or troubles you periodically? _____

· · ·

*L*ist 3 questions that assume you can make things better
and are designed to prompt action.

_____

_____

_____

*W*hat question could you ask yourself that might
prompt you to take actions?

_____

_____

_____

_____

*W*hat is one thing, however small, you could do
today that might help you address that issue?

_____

*L*ist 5 skills and resources you already have to deal with
this situation.

_____

_____

_____

_____

_____

*I*f you're struggling to list 5, what are some things you
could do over the next few months to change that?

_____

_____

. . .

*O*ver the next year?

----

*L*ist 5 small things you could do to put yourself in a better position to address your concerns or take the actions you listed above.

Chapter Nine

I AM I SAID: PROS AND CONS OF AFFIRMATIONS

So I came up with my affirmation "I am creative. I am an author". At the time, I was not creative and I was not an author.

- Joanna Penn, *The Creative Penn*

You may also want to rewrite your inner life and use language to feel happier and calmer through affirmations. This technique, in my view, has some drawbacks, which I'll talk about below. But many people find affirmations — positive statements that certain things have happened or exist in your life right now — enhance their lives and chances of success.

An affirmation can be about actual good things in your life or about things that you aspire to.

If you hope to write your first novel this year, for instance, but you haven't started yet you might say aloud or write an affirmation such as "I am a novelist. I finished a great novel."

If you're feeling very nervous about public speaking you might say or write, "I am a strong, confident speaker audiences love."

For some people writing or saying these types of statements encourages them and sets them moving toward that goal.

Other people's brains respond by contradicting the statements. For instance, if you say you're a good public speaker a voice in the back of your mind might insist, "No I'm not. I'm terrible at public speaking. My hands shake, my voice is too quiet, and I'm afraid the audience members will start talking amongst themselves and ignore me."

If you fall in the latter camp, you may want to go back to asking questions. Rather than an affirmation you could ask, "How can I become a good public speaker?"

Odds are, you'll come up with lots of great answers.

You might need to practice in front of a mirror, prepare your remarks and rehearse them twice as much as you do now, or simply take speaking engagement after speaking engagement until you get good at it. Or you could do research into how other great public speakers developed their skills.

You can also create affirmations about your emotional state. These are the types that work best for me. Even if I am anxious it sometimes helps me to say, "I am calm, confident, and happy."

In addition, affirmations can reinforce things you know are true or feel confident you can achieve but aren't energized about right now. So if you are, in fact, a great personal assistant but you're nervous about a new job it can help to affirm to yourself that you are excellent at organizing, managing databases, and dealing with people (or whatever skills you know you'll need).

I personally find writing affirmations works better than speaking.

If I speak them my brain often disputes them. If I write them, though, I think my brain sees them more as goals or aspirations and sets about working towards them.

Labeling affirmations goals can be a great way to respond if that little voice in the back of your head tends to undercut your statements.

If you say your "goal" is to write a novel this year your brain is less likely to tell you that you haven't done it or can't do it. Calling it a goal also implies that you will take steps to get there.

If you're unsure you can experiment with affirmations in a few areas of your life and see if they help you feel better and happier.

In the next chapter we'll talk about another way to feel better about life as it is right now, whether you use affirmations or not. But first:

*W*rite 3 or 4 affirmations now. (You can write ones that specifically address your writing goals, or inner peace, or income, or family — whatever you like.)

----

*P*ost them in places where you'll see them regularly.

*O*ver the next few weeks pay attention to whether these posted affirmations make you more likely to take steps to turn your affirmations into reality.

Chapter Ten

FOUR STEPS TO FEELING FANTASTIC

The truth is, there's no better time to be happy than right now. If not now, when?

-- Richard Carlson, *Don't Sweat The Small Stuff...And It's All Small Stuff: Simple Ways To Keep The Little Things From Taking Over Your Life*

*I*t's hard to feel anxious and grateful at the same time. One emotion tends to override the other.

When you're gripped by anxiety, though, you may feel it's impossible to imagine you can shift from fear to gratitude. Or that it's safe to do so.

So how to do it? Here are four steps:

- Start small
- Write it down
- Multiply By Five
- Share

If these steps for immersing yourself in gratitude are the only things you adopt from this book, in my opinion it will increase your happiness, and decrease your anxiety, more than you can imagine.

START SMALL

The key is to find real things to be grateful for in your life right now. If you're in the middle of a truly difficult time that can be a challenge. Which is why we start small.

For instance, you're reading this book, so right there is something to be grateful for. You were able to buy or borrow a book to read or listen to.

Right now you can feel grateful for that. You can use your imagination to remember the look and feel of a book that changed your life. You can use your analytic mind to pinpoint how a skill or fact you learned from an article helped your career or improved your relationships. You can remember the moments that inspired you to become a writer.

While you're doing that, at least for those moments, it's pretty hard not to feel good.

Also, like anxiety, gratitude feeds on itself and gets easier with practice. The more you look for and note things you're grateful for, however small, the more of them you'll see.

WRITE IT

Writing down what we feel grateful for fixes it more firmly in our minds. It also creates a record of the good things in our lives to look back on when we need it. And, as with any other kind of writing, the more detail, the more real it seems and the more fixed it becomes in our hearts and minds.

For instance, if you're grateful because your cousin, whom you don't see often, came into town and you had a nice dinner don't just write *Dinner with my cousin.*

Instead, use your memory and writing skills to expand on the parts of the evening. Make them vivid by using all your senses:

- *Spaghetti came out just right — the fresh tomatoes with it made it taste fantastic*
- *Shared stories about our parents — heard ones I never knew about my mom — helped me understand her better*
- *So enjoyed the cold root beer – reminds me of summer vacation as a kid and going to A&W as a treat*
- *Warmth of the fireplace looked beautiful and made me feel cheerful and relaxed*
- *Fresh-baked chocolate chip cookies for dessert made the whole apartment smell great and feel warm and cozy; loved the dark chocolate for the chips*

Even if you're also right now worried about paying your bills, a family member's illness, or a relationship, it'd be hard not to feel good while you're actually writing a description like that.

MULTIPLY BY FIVE

You can write or think about something you're grateful for whenever you start feeling low or worried. But being more proactive about it is a stronger recipe for happiness and the best way to make it a habit. My goal isn't only to feel less anxious or depressed, it's to feel happy, calm, and excited about life most of the time.

Part of doing that is writing each morning in a journal five things that I'm grateful for.

Finding five things pushes me to look beyond the obvious and truly see how much is good in my life. It also ensures I'll re-experience those good things and makes it feel like I have double the amount of them in my life.

I like to do this in the morning because if I do happen to

awaken feeling anxious or sad, by the time I've written five things I almost always feel better. If I find only one, on the other hand, I can jot it down without really focusing on it or changing my state of mind.

If you don't have time for that sort of morning writing, and there are definitely times when I haven't had it, don't worry. Gratitude writing is flexible.

On a busy day, despite what I said above about detailing dinner with your cousin, you can list five things quickly in a shorthand form. Though you haven't spent a lot of time, you've at least noticed those five things and written them.

Which means you're still getting your brain in the habit of picking out what's great in your life.

On a day when you have a little more time you can re-envision, re-experience, and write a few lines about each one or at least delve at length into one or two of them. If there's a morning where you have more free time, you can write each of the five things in depth. (If mornings are too busy, you can do that on your lunch hour or before you go to sleep.)

As with every strategy in this book, use it only if you find it helps you, and modify it if you need to.

If you find you're struggling to find five things, stick with one for a while unless and until it feels natural to add to your list. And if you feel worse after this exercise or during it, set it aside. It's not for everyone.

SHARE

Assuming you are writing what you feel grateful about, sharing that with other people can further increase your feelings of well-being and happiness.

It can also add to your life far into the future.

The other night I mentioned to one of my nieces that I had started writing in a gratitude journal again. She told me something I had completely forgotten. Apparently I was thinking of things I was grateful for during the time after my parents died. One day I emailed her that she was one of the people I was so grateful was in my life and I told her why. As that was over a decade ago, I don't remember specifically what I said and neither does she. But she remembers that I told her I felt grateful for her and it meant a lot to her. It's one of many reasons that we remain close over the years.

So consider taking it a step further and, if you're grateful for a person, let that person know.

Finally, whether or not you write down what you're grateful for, it's a wonderful question to ask yourself while you shower or make dinner or clean the house.

*L*ist 3-5 things you're grateful for right now.

_____
_____
_____
_____
_____

*A*re people on that list? _____

*W*ould you feel comfortable telling one of them about your feelings of gratitude?

_____

. . .

*I*f so, or if you're a little uncomfortable but think it might help to do it, send a text, email, or letter or call and share your feelings. How did you feel afterwards?

_____

_____

_____

Chapter Eleven

WORDS TO ENHANCE OUR LIVES

What does it mean to relax?....most people will answer in a way that suggests that relaxing is something you plan to do later — you do it on a vacation, in a hammock, or when you get everything done. This implies, of course, that most other times (the other 95 percent of your life) should be spent nervous, agitated, rushed, and frenzied.

     -- Richard Carlson, *Don't Sweat The Small Stuff...And It's All Small Stuff: Simple Ways To Keep The Little Things From Taking Over Your Life*

*I*n addition to the questions we ask, how we feel — happy, anxious, sad, stressed, angry, calm — arises from the words we use to describe our lives.

That is great news for writers.

We're used to thoughtfully choosing our words. We do it all the time when we write and especially when we rewrite because we know how much difference a single word can make.

Describing a person as "tall" has a different effect then calling her "towering." Calling her a "beanpole" or a "giant" also creates a radically different image and feeling. Yet all of those words could in theory be used to describe someone who was 7 feet tall.

In the same way we can choose words that enhance our health and happiness.

We can start by being as accurate as possible in what we say.

A TERRIBLE SPIRAL

Why does accurate language increase the chances we'll feel calm and happy? Shouldn't we be using "positive" language instead?

As to the first question, many of us, especially if we're prone to anxiety, unintentionally use language that causes us to spiral further into the abyss.

If you're already feeling anxious or down and get stuck in a traffic jam, you might describe the drive as terrible and lament how where you live has become so crowded it's intolerable. You'll likely feel anxious that you won't get to your destination on time and talk through in your mind all the bad consequences if you're late. Whether you're actually late or not, you'll feel stressed by the time you arrive.

In a good mood, though, you might look ahead, see a section of construction causing the delay, and think, "How frustrating. I better leave earlier tomorrow." Even if you're concerned about being late, you'll probably be realistic about what will happen if you are. And if you do arrive on time, you'll forget about the drive quickly.

The great thing is that you can choose your words deliberately in a way that makes you less likely to feel worse and more likely to feel calmer and happier.

As to the second question, I'm not suggesting using language to minimize anxious or discouraged feelings (or what's actually happening) or to always be positive.

That's because when it comes to anxiety, for me at least, purposely denying or minimizing the feeling or situation often makes me feel worse. In those moments, I feel sure in my gut there is something really wrong or that there's a strong chance there could be. Pretending that's not so only makes my mind insist that there is a problem. A real problem. A serious one. Maybe an insurmountable one.

Also, I grew up being taught to ignore or discount or minimize my feelings. I spent a lot of years and money in therapy learning to recognize how I feel and appreciating it. I'm not willing to go back to being out of touch with my feelings even if it might help me manage anxiety in the short term.

So what's the answer?

ACCURATE WORDS

There's a difference between minimizing feelings and situations and accurately describing them.

Imagine your boss says nothing when you say good morning to her. Instead, she goes straight into her office and shuts her door.

If you're already feeling anxious you'll probably describe her as ignoring you and slamming her door. If you argued with her the day before you'll probably start wondering if she's angry with you. If you're like me, next you'll start thinking about how the company hasn't been doing so well. What if you're next on the chopping block?

If you take a breath, though, and use words that accurately describe what happened you'll say your boss walked past you and closed her door without speaking.

From that you might conclude she had other things on her mind and didn't notice you.

Or perhaps she was late for a conference call. If you're concerned about friction between you, you can ask later if anything was wrong, but you won't spend the day dwelling on it.

Or let's say, as recently happened to me, I fall and break two bones in my foot. Let's further say that one of those bones is one of the most significant ones on which you put most of your weight, which means multiple casts and a long time off my feet. Also, imagine that because I'm self-employed I have a very high insurance deductible. (All of which is true.)

I could say that breaking my foot was a disaster. I could say that I'll go broke paying the doctor and emergency room bills because the charges are horrendous and outrageous. I could also say that I spent forever off of my feet, that while I was on crutches I was exhausted, and that it took a huge amount of effort to do every day things so I'll never finish my next novel.

All those things are guaranteed to raise anxiety about my physical well-being, my finances, and my work.

While there are real and genuine concerns I'm expressing, those statements are not accurate.

Yes, doctor, physical therapy, and hospital bills are expensive. And I do have a high deductible. But when I became self-employed I knew that was a risk I was taking. Because of that, before leaving my job I saved money just in case I had a health emergency. Using the just-in-case money and then some is no fun, and it does mean being a lot more careful with money this year and next year. But accurately stating that I used up the money I put aside years ago just in case is a lot more accurate, and less anxiety-provoking, than saying I owe a fortune or went broke.

Saying how grateful I am that I can buy health insurance, which saved me from paying ten times more in total than I did, is also accurate. Those words make me feel a lot better about my care and how much I spent than talking about how much everything costs. So does telling people how thankful I am that I was to be able to see a doctor at a good hospital, as I realize many people don't have access to that.

But let's say I didn't have that money put aside.

Saying I'd go broke wouldn't be accurate or help me deal with the medical bills. It would be more accurate and helpful to say I'd be paying off bills for a long time. Or that when I'm better I may need to look for a more traditional job with better health insurance or work that pays more.

Would I like that idea?

No. But it wouldn't be the end of the world.

Similarly, it was not accurate to say I would never finish my next novel. It was accurate to say that I'd hoped to release three to five books last year, and instead I released two.

It's also accurate to say I feel a little sad and anxious about writing more slowly than I'd planned.

That statement acknowledges my feelings. But it doesn't make the situation worse than it is. It makes it more likely I'll feel calm enough to get more done now that I'm doing so much better.

By accurately describing my feelings I put myself in a better position to deal with whatever it is I'm facing. And I'm putting myself in a good frame of mind to use the types of questions from Chapters 7 and 8 to move forward from here.

As I'll talk more about in a moment, we can also use language to focus on what makes us feel good and happy.

Before you read on, though, these prompts may help you get used to revising what you say about challenges you face to be more accurate:

*R*emember a recent difficult situation that you told people about using words like "awful" or "terrible." List the specific words you used to describe what happened.

_____

_____

. . .

*H*ow did you describe your feelings?

_____

_____

*F*or each adjective or adverb you used, come up with four or five alternate words that are more accurate.

_____

_____

_____

_____

_____

*D*id that change how you feel? _____

FOCUS

What we dwell on in detail through our words often dictates where our hearts and minds will be. It also determines the quality of our inner lives. It's hard to feel peaceful or happy if we're immersing ourselves in memories or moments that upset us, trigger our fears, or leave us feeling angry or depressed.

So how do we change our focus?

Think of it as if you were writing a scene.

When we want the reader to feel certain things we include details drawn from our senses. We describe those details in ways that create a mood.

To elicit a feeling of fear we might describe sudden noises, intense or offensive smells, sweating palms, a racing heart, rushing in the ears, glaring lights, or dry lips.

For sadness, we might describe a street as full of shadows and hone in on dark areas between the streetlights. If we do write about a light, it's a stark glare, not a warm yellow glow.

Similarly, describing a living room in winter sets a much different tone if we focus on the wind rattling the window panes rather than a fire crackling and a radiator steaming.

The verbs we choose matter, too.

Do the radiators steam or hiss? Does the wind smack the window panes, rattle them, slam against them, threaten to shatter them? Or does it whisper through the yard or caress a woman's face?

As in fiction, so go our lives.

Put another way, altering how we describe our past, present, and anticipated future can change how we experience it.

To put this idea into practice, try making a habit of remembering and describing to yourself and others in detail what's good in your life, no matter how small or large. You'll re-experience it in more depth and expand your good feelings. The more you do that, the more you'll be able to use those retellings and memories to replace unpleasant experiences and memories.

That's not to say you should ignore situations that upset you or feelings of anger, sadness, or fear. But if you are accurate in how you describe them and don't make them larger than they are, it'll be easier to handle them. And if revisiting those life circumstances or feelings doesn't help you, you'll be more able to leave them in the past.

*D*escribe something from the past that raises anxious, sad, or angry feelings.

· · ·

*I*s it something you can do anything about now?

_____

*I*s there anything you can learn from it?

_____

*I*f so, describe it as accurately as possible.

_____

_____

_____

*W*hat's your plan for dealing with this event?

_____

_____

_____

*D*escribe something that happened to you in the past (recent or distant) that made you feel wonderful.

_____

_____

_____

*R*ewrite your description adding more detail. Include what you saw, heard, felt, smelled, and tasted if possible.

_____
_____
_____
_____
_____
_____
_____
_____

Chapter Twelve

FEEDING OUR MINDS

*H*ow we feel depends on more than how we describe what's in our minds or what we ask ourselves. It also turns on what we feed into our minds.

I was first introduced to this idea in college when my boyfriend at the time started having panic attacks. The serious kind that feel like a heart attack. When he went to the emergency room the ER doc kept asking him what drugs he had taken. The answer was none. His body and brain were doing this all on their own.

After months of seeing doctors and undergoing tests for physical causes he finally saw a psychiatrist who told him he was having panic attacks and helped him figure out how to deal with it.

One of the first things that doctor told him to do was stop watching the news. Books and articles I read later on anxiety and panic attacks seconded that advice.

INFORMATION WITHOUT FEAR

Television headlines or news alerts in particular tend to heighten fear. They suggest worst-case scenarios. They hone in on conflict. It's what gets people to tune in and keeps them watching or checking their messages. Particularly now that we have a twenty-four hour news cycle and multiple venues competing for our attention, the ones that send our adrenaline surging often garner the most attention.

Nothing about that is good for a calm, happy life.

I'm not suggesting anyone should become an uninformed person. I am suggesting that there are better and calmer ways to stay informed. You can find thoughtful, well-reasoned articles in newspapers and on the Internet that provide information without sensationalism.

Another option is to subscribe to a single email that rounds up the most important news. Choose one that includes information rather than hyped headlines and that covers topics about things you truly need to know.

You might also, or instead, choose a friend who stays well-informed and doesn't become anxious the way you do.

That person can fill you in on anything major that's happening without the unnecessary drama.

Similarly, if you listen to podcasts, try to choose not only good content but a style of delivery that encourages you.

My favorite writing and publishing podcast is The Creative Penn. It covers tons of helpful information, but many websites and podcasts offer solid publishing and marketing advice to authors. I listen to this one more than any other because Joanna Penn sounds unfailingly upbeat (though not so upbeat it depresses me if I'm feeling blue) and hopeful. I'm sure she has her dark days, but she shares from a place of hope and optimism, and I need that.

Other people may prefer a different type of voice or outlook. It's up to you.

THE STORIES YOU CHOOSE

Likewise, think about how you feel when you read certain types of books or watch TV shows or movies. In particular, notice how your body feels as you read or watch.

- Do you tense?
- Do you feel like dragging yourself into bed and sleeping for days?
- Do you find yourself feeling worse about your life?

If so, try feeding your mind and spirit something else.

I write suspense novels, mysteries, and thrillers. But after my parents' deaths, I found reading books that delved into the minds of killers, covered multiple murders, or described violence in graphic detail upset and depressed me. In the past, I hadn't loved those aspects of the books, but I'd enjoyed the overall pace, the shifting viewpoints, and the resolution, which usually involved some sort of justice.

Though my parents died due to someone else's choice to drink and drive, not because someone set out to harm them, the books raised too many disturbing feelings for me.

I shifted my reading to suspenseful books that were less graphic or that focused more on efforts to solve crimes than on the people who caused them.

For related reasons I usually avoid family sagas where everyone is unlikable, has deep-seated issues that cause disturbing behaviors, or acts unhinged. Those types of stories send me down a dark rabbit hole. I want books that resolve happily or with some hope at the end. Many literary novels, for me, ramble into dark places and never get out, so they are usually not my first choice.

You may react differently to the books I love or to the books I find troubling. And what makes you feel good to read may be different from what you watch and may change over time. The point is to choose what's best for you right now.

SETTING THE TONE

You can also seek out content that will enhance your happiness and peace of mind.

I often start my day by reading a page or two of *Don't Sweat The Small Stuff...And It's All Small Stuff: Simple Ways To Keep The Little Things From Taking Over Your Life*, particularly during times when I'm juggling too many responsibilities or am feeling anxious.

I heard of the book long before I read it, but avoided it because the title made me think it was about learning to be a slacker. It's not. It's about how to be relaxed and happy while still working hard and achieving goals, something that I'd thought impossible. As you probably noticed, a lot of the quotes in this book came from *Don't Sweat The Small Stuff*.

Right now I'm relistening to *The One Thing: The Surprisingly Simple Truth Behind Extraordinary Results*, which helps me stay energized and excited about writing and finishing my books and putting effort into advertising and business.

You can also start your morning by listening to an encouraging or energizing podcast, audiobook, or radio program or reading a website that helps you relax or makes you feel ready to start your day.

Even if you listen or read for 5-10 minutes it can help you start the day in a good frame of mind.

*W*hat books, articles, podcasts, or blogs have you read that help you remain calm, feel happier, or enjoy life more?

---

*I*f you can't think of any, or if you only listed one or two, when can you set aside 15 minutes to find at least one (or one more)?

---

*W*hat types of books (fiction or non-fiction) do you feel the best while you're reading?

---

*W*hat movies or series do you feel the best after you've watched?

---

*A*re there public figures or speakers you find inspiring? Which ones?

Chapter Thirteen

ONE THING AT A TIME

Task switching exacts a cost few even realize they're paying.

You can do two things at once but you can't focus effectively on two things at once.

— Gary Keller, *The One Thing: The Surprisingly Simple Truth Behind Extraordinary Results*

a lot of this book deals with language because that's the way, as writers, we communicate with our readers. It's also key to how we think, which is, in essence, how we communicate with ourselves.

But our minds can improve our happiness, and lessen our stress and anxiety, in other ways. Specifically, though mindfulness, which I talk about below, and visualization, which I'll cover in the next chapter.

MINDFULNESS

An in-depth study of mindfulness could take decades. For many people, it's part of a spiritual or religious practice. I'm covering it, though, only as it relates to feeling calmer and happier regardless of your beliefs (or lack thereof) in any sort of higher power or spiritual realm.

What is mindfulness?

My hands-on personal definition: Paying attention to what you're doing and nothing else.

If you're washing the dishes, you're washing dishes. That's it. You're not also figuring out how you'll pay this month's rent, watching a favorite television episode in the background, or talking on the phone. (Or all three, for that matter.)

In other words, mindfulness is like single-tasking.

Most of us, though, are always looking to do multiple things at once. We brush our teeth while listening to the news while standing on one foot to improve our balance. (Wait, is that just me? Well, you get the idea.)

For writers, keeping our minds on a repetitive task can be especially challenging. We're used to using that time to spin out plot ideas, ask ourselves questions about our characters, or write essays or op-eds in our heads.

You may still want to use some of your time that way. If you're working full-time at other work, paid or unpaid, it may be the only way to make progress on your writing.

But some of the time try shifting to single-tasking.

To go back to dishwashing, when you pick up a sponge feel it in your hand as you wash a dish. Smell the detergent. Feel the water running over your skin. If your mind drifts to something else, gently return your thoughts to the dishes, the water, the soap.

That's all you do.

At first this way of thinking only about what you are doing can feel boring, especially if it's a task that you do often and don't enjoy. If you stick with it, though, you may discover you relax. That it's a relief to do only one thing.

That's in part because when you stop and simply brush your teeth or fold the laundry you're signaling your mind and body that you are not, in fact, in such a rush that you can't so much as fold a towel without needing to multi-task.

I found this approach tremendously helpful during times of intense anxiety.

When I moved home from California, many mornings I felt as if I couldn't get through the next moment let alone the next day, week, or year. I remember sitting at my parents' kitchen table, knowing I needed to eat and get ready for my temporary office job, yet feeling overwhelmed by anxiety and unable to move.

And I thought, "Okay, walk to the cabinet."

Once I got to the cabinet, I told myself to get out a cereal box. I did that. Then I got out a bowl. Then I filled it. And so on. It's how I got to work each day.

Happily, since then I've rarely had to break things down that much. But there are lots of times I'll find my body tightening and my thoughts racing. Rather than try to figure out what's wrong, for a few minutes I'll do my best to focus on what I'm doing and only what I'm doing. As I ease into my day one step at a time, the anxiety lessens and things get easier.

If you're skeptical about whether mindfulness can feel good, consider how you feel when you're completely absorbed in your writing. Everything else falls away. Words appear on the page almost by magic. You're immersed in your story or the flow of words.

It's the reason most of us love to write. We love experiencing those very moments.

That's mindfulness.

With practice, you can get there more and more often, not only when you write. And you don't need to do anything special to practice.

Just do
one thing
at a time.

Keeping that in mind, let's move on to visualization.

Chapter Fourteen

VISUALIZATION

The clearer and stronger your intention, the more quickly and easily your creative visualization will work.

— Shakti Gawain, *Creative Visualization: Use the Power of Your Imagination to Create What You Want in Your Life*

When you visualize, you imagine a scene or series of scenes. You can use it to help you feel calmer and happier and/or to achieve particular goals.

DECREASING ANXIETY

When I struggled with social anxiety, I used relaxation exercises (which I'll get to in a moment) to reach a calmer state of mind. I then imagined myself talking with someone with whom I had previously felt anxious. Or I imagined myself giving a presentation or arguing in court.

I heard myself speaking at a normal rate of speed, not rushing through my words as most of us do when we feel nervous. I imagined in detail how I looked and felt (well dressed, smiling, jaw relaxed, no sweating or flushing, and standing comfortably without fidgeting). The scene around me included details from all my senses. I saw other people, too, and imagined them reacting as they would in my ideal world. Because I had already put myself in a calm state of mind, I usually was able to imagine the interaction without becoming very anxious.

After practicing these interactions over and over in my mind, I began to feel more comfortable doing them in real life.

None of which means I immediately felt relaxed the first time I gave a talk in front of fifty people despite that I'd imagined it. But it helped, and the more I practiced in real life the better I got at it. If I had a rough moment where I became anxious and my voice shook or my palms sweated, I felt discouraged, but I didn't let it stop me. I kept talking or interacting. Then I went home and practiced visualizing it again and again while calm.

Because of visualization, I became so much more comfortable with public speaking and interacting that I became a lawyer and later a professor. I now enjoy arguing in court, teaching, and public speaking. These are some of my favorite things to do.

HAPPINESS AND GOALS

In addition, visualization can improve general happiness. Partly that's because we need to figure out what we believe would make us happy in order to visualize it.

When I had the repetitive stress injury and struggled to find my first paralegal job, I visualized my ideal work situation. To do that, I had to both narrow down and expand exactly what I wanted. I identified not only what I didn't want — lots of typing — but what I'd want whether or not my injury existed. And I found that job, down to having an office of my own, doing a lot of legal research and writing, and interacting directly with clients.

In that sense, visualization relates to affirmations, as you are imagining you've already achieved your goal.

I personally find visualization more motivating, though. I'm imagining where I want to be rather than merely saying I'm already there. It's like a vivid daydream. It helps convince me I can achieve something that seems difficult or far off.

A caveat:

I've heard about studies suggesting visualizing can rob you of motivation. The theory is that we can feel so great imagining our success that we are less motivated to do the hard work to reach that goal. I've not found that to be true for me, but you should pay attention to the results when you visualize.

If you find you are less motivated, you may want to skip this technique. Or limit visualization to helping you relax rather than to achieving other types of goals.

HOW TO DO IT

I use these three steps to visualize:

1. Choose what to visualize
2. Relax
3. Shut your eyes and imagine

STEP ONE: WHAT TO VISUALIZE

What you'll imagine depends on what you want to achieve.

When I was writing my first couple novels I did short visualizations where I'd imagine the pages of my novel coming out of my printer. I didn't picture specific words, just hundreds of sheets of printed pages shooting out of the printer. That helped me believe that I could finish the entire novel before I'd written a page or when I felt stuck in the middle.

I also saw myself at my desk typing my novel at my keyboard or writing longhand in a notebook.

For some non-writing examples, you could:

- Imagine your boss telling you you're being promoted
- See yourself performing tasks at a new job
- Picture a particular figure for your bank balance
- Imagine in detail the vacation you'll take when you finish a project
- See yourself doing well at a piano recital

If your goal is more general, such as to improve your happiness and peacefulness or decrease stress, you'll want to choose a favorite place where you feel good. It can be a real one you've been to or one you imagine.

Mine is lying in a hammock. The sun is shining and the grass and trees around me are lush and green. Beyond me the ocean waves crash on rocks under a clear blue sky.

By visiting your relaxed place through visualization, you can experience the feelings you'd have if you were able to physically go there.

STEP TWO: RELAX

Before you visualize, you will want to get into a relaxed frame of mind. One way is to try a quick relaxation exercise.

These few moments really can make a difference. But remember, as with any exercise, you should check with your doctor first before trying it and/or modify or skip it if that's what's best for you.

Exercise 1
This one can be done anywhere. It takes less than three minutes.

Sit, stand, or lie down and do the following:

- Shut your eyes
- Breathe in to the count of two through your nose, allowing your diaphragm to expand as you do

- Hold your breath for the count of two
- Exhale to the count of two, contracting your diaphragm
- Repeat each step to the count of four, then six, then eight, then ten, and then twelve if you can.
- If you can't hold your breath that long or you don't feel good when you do, stop at an earlier count. (You'll likely get better at it as you practice.)

This exercise pushes us to truly exhale and empty our lungs. Exhaling is particularly important because when we become anxious, we tend not to exhale completely. We're always keeping a certain amount of air in our lungs and breathing in a shallow way that tends to add to our anxiety.

When I ran my own law firm I used to do this exercise while heating a cup of tea in the microwave, which took two minutes, whether or not I planned to try any visualizing.

It had an unexpected side benefit. At the time I had a lot of digestion problems. They eased significantly when I started doing this exercise regularly. I'm guessing that I had been swallowing air when I felt anxious, which was adding to my stomach issues.

Exercise 2

An even quicker relaxation exercise is to simply breathe in to the count of two and breathe out to the count of two slowly five times. It's good to shut your eyes while doing it because you block out everything else.

Exercise 3

If you have a little more time before you visualize you can try a whole body relaxation. (This one also can help if you're having trouble falling asleep.)

If it's daytime, I usually light a candle with a scent I find relaxing. (At night I'll put a scented candle near my bed but leave it unlit for safety reasons.)

I lie on my bed or the floor. If my body is otherwise feeling well, I start with my feet and tense each body part, then relax it, working my way through all the muscles.

So I would tense my toes and then let them relax, tense the arches and tops of my feet and relax them, tense my ankles and relax them and so on. When I'm done, I tense my entire body and relax it.

After that, without tensing, I simply focus on each body part. I hear my own voice in my head saying something like, "My toes are relaxing. My toes are very relaxed. My toes are as relaxed as I've ever felt them. They are so relaxed I feel them floating." I take a moment to imagine my toes floating, then move to the next part of the foot and so on.

If it helps, you can record yourself talking through relaxing each part of your body in advance, then listen and follow your own voice's prompts.

I learned this exercise when I had tendinitis and a lot of pain in my hands and arms. By the time I got to my hands most of my body was relaxed and I did feel my hands were floating. Sometimes my entire body felt weightless. It often was the only ten or so minutes of the day when my hands and arms didn't hurt.

The relaxation exercise kept me from constantly tensing my muscles for probably an hour or so afterwards.

STEP THREE: VISUALIZE

Once you're relaxed, however you get there, sit or lie down and shut your eyes. If you're concerned about falling asleep or you have limited time, you can set a timer before you start to visualize. Just make sure you have an alarm sound that's enough to awaken you but doesn't startle you.

Now imagine the scene you decided on beforehand. Engage all your senses.

If you're imagining your finished novel, for instance, feel how the cover feels under your hands.

Is it smooth? How does the paper feel?

See the words on the page.

Is the paper bright white? Cream colored? Does the type stand out?

How does the book smell?

See yourself holding the book.

Are you smiling? Are your shoulders relaxed? Is anyone there with you?

If you've visualized your calming place, relax and enjoy being there.

Whatever you visualized, you can replay the scene as often and for as long as you want.

*W*hich relaxation exercise sounds most appealing to you?

_____

*H*ow do you feel when you do it?

_____

_____

*I*f you want to try visualization, what are some goals you want to imagine yourself achieving?

_____

_____

_____

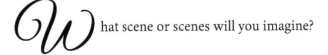

*W*hat scene or scenes will you imagine?

_____
_____
_____

escribe aloud to yourself what you'll see, hear, touch, taste, and/or smell.

Chapter Fifteen

WRITING, FEAR, AND TIME

*T*his is not a book on time management. But I do want to talk about time.

Because often the feeling that we lack enough time to write masks fear. Why do I believe this?

Because for decades I've interacted with other writers in classes, workshops, seminars, and socially. What I've noticed is that many writers finish books or stories or articles despite significant demands on their time. It may take longer than they'd hoped, and they may shift the scale of their projects. (Maybe writing short stories or blog posts rather than a novel during times when they need to work, raise a small child, and care for an aging parent or all three at once.)

But they do write and they do finish. And they start another project.

On the flipside, over the years I've known many writers who plan to write when their life changes. When their kids are grown. When they retire. When they can afford to take some time off in between jobs.

Yet when that event finally occurs most still don't find time for writing. Or they do set aside some time, but they stare at the blank page or screen and eventually walk away.

I believe this happens because, whether aware of it or not, we harbor a lot of fear about writing.

(The above observations are not meant to minimize very real challenges we all sometimes face in scheduling writing time. You can get help with that in any of a vast number of books that overflow virtual and physical bookshelves, including one of mine, The One-Year Novelist: A Week-By-Week Guide To Writing Your Novel In One Year (Writing As A Second Career Book 3).

You can also search the Internet for advice. If the real issue is how you use your time, you'll likely find a system that will work for you.)

Most of our fear comes down to one question:

- What if I devote all these hours to writing my novel (or story or poem or non-fiction book) and I don't finish it, or I do finish but no one buys it or likes it?

Okay, that's a very long question.

Maybe it ought to be two questions. Either way, though, your brain likely responds with these types of answers:

1. I'll have wasted time I could have/should have spent on something else
2. I'll discover I can't write
3. I'll lose my identity as a writer
4. No one will buy my finished product
5. People will judge my work
6. People will criticize me
7. I'll fail

Dwelling on the limits on our time allows us to sidestep these fears. Instead we can imagine that someday our other responsibilities will lessen or disappear. Then we'll write, and it will be wonderful.

It doesn't help that some of these fears quite possibly will come true, some almost certainly will, and only a few are entirely baseless.

Once you're aware of your fear, though, you can handle it as you do other anxious thoughts using the techniques in this book.

But because it's writing, let's delve into each a little further.

ON "WASTING" TIME (FEAR 1)

Fear No. 1 is never completely baseless.

Spending time on one pursuit means opting not to spend it on something else. That has real consequences. You're gambling that you'll be better off (in one way or another) spending your time writing than doing anything else.

If this fear plagues you, ask yourself what you want not only from writing but from life. If you feel that another path will be more apt to make you happier, that's okay. You can make writing less of a priority and pursue that path. It doesn't mean you won't or can't write.

For one thing, you may change course later down the road. Also, sometimes allowing yourself to purposefully choose other things over writing frees up your mind to write. Writing becomes fun again rather than a chore.

On the other hand, if writing appears likely to satisfy your goals, or you love it so much you're willing to risk forgoing other aspects of life, revisit Chapters 7 and 8 on questions. See if you can reframe what you're asking yourself to help you move forward happily with your writing.

To ease yourself into writing instead of other things try setting a date to check in on your progress. Promise yourself that in three months, or six, or a year, you'll carefully consider how you feel about what you've skipped doing so you could write.

You may find you don't miss those other things at all. Or that writing is its own reward. Or that you've made so much progress you're ready to devote another six months.

If not, you can adjust going forward to better suit your life.

Finally, if you love writing as much as I suspect you do (because you're still reading), you may want to redefine what you mean by "wasting time." I've loved every minute I've spent writing, including on novels that I've never published. I don't feel I wasted time on any of it.

If you can reassure yourself that the time won't be wasted, you'll free yourself to write more.

WRITING AND YOUR IDENTITY (FEARS 2 AND 3)

The next two fears — you'll discover you can't write and you'll lose your identity as a writer — are related. Many people are afraid they'll start a writing project and never finish. Or they'll plan to start but never will. Or they won't hit some benchmark for number of pages written or money earned that in their minds equals being a "real" writer.

It may help to realize there's nothing mystic about writing that causes these concerns. This fear, also known as the imposter syndrome, operates everywhere.

I once talked with a criminal prosecutor who'd been practicing law about three years, as I had at the time. He told me he didn't feel like a "real lawyer" because his work didn't involve the type of legal analysis, research, and writing that we all spent a lot of time learning in law school (and which made up the bulk of my practice). I told him I didn't feel like a real lawyer because I hadn't tried a case yet. A personal injury trial lawyer I talked with that same week said he didn't feel like a real lawyer because he tried auto accident cases, not criminal cases.

We were all licensed in the State of Illinois. We were all making our living practicing law, and we all were respected by our colleagues. But somehow our minds had this idea that someone else out there was the real thing and we were playacting or at least still learning.

So if your definition of a "real writer" excludes you the first thing to do is change it.

For instance, if "real" to you is someone who has sold at least 100 novels, or 100,000, you can redefine it as someone who writes. (Which, by the way, is a pretty good dictionary definition of writer.) If you write – whether you finish what you write, sell it, publish it or not – you are a writer. You cannot lose that identity.

This change doesn't mean you can't still aspire to sell 100 books or 1,000 or 100,000 or whatever else you want to do. Those goals are just that – goals. You can pursue them with all your heart and soul. Just don't make achieving them define you.

But what if you fear you'll find out you "can't" write?

As with what being a writer means, you're likely putting a lot of weight on what "I can write" means.

To me, it means I can type or write words on a page that come together into sentences. That's it. If you're reading this book, you know how to do that. At the very least, you can take one of my sentences, rephrase it, and write it down.

I'm not trying to be flip here. And I can hear you saying that's not what you meant.

I get it. You don't literally mean you can't write. You likely mean you fear you'll discover you can't write well.

Guess what? Maybe you can't. When I got my first guitar, I couldn't play it. But I learned. And I practiced. And practiced. And practiced. For years.

Writing is no different. Like anything else, most people who seem like "naturals" got so good at it by doing it over and over. You may never see it, but their early writing was almost certainly terrible. The more they wrote — and the more you write — the better the writing will be.

So try going back to the chapters on questions and consider how you might change your questions about being a writer and writing well.

For example, rather than asking *What if I can't write?* you might ask:

- *How can I become a better writer?*
- *What can I do for ten minutes today that could become part of a novel?*
- *What area of writing (plot, line editing, characterization, etc.) do I want to focus on this month?*
- *What story am I most excited about telling?*

No matter your answers, simply asking and answering will go a long way toward feeling less fearful.

BUYING, JUDGING, CRITICIZING, FAILING (FEARS 4-7)

The last four fears I listed are different forms of fear of how you'll feel if others judge you in a negative way. The fear that people won't buy your writing (Fear 4), that people will judge your work or will criticize you as an author (Fears 5 and 6), and that you'll fail (Fear 7) reflect how you're afraid you'll feel if you put your writing out into the world.

Here's the tough thing about Fears 4-6. In one form or another, they will happen.

No matter how many people buy your book, some people won't. Because they don't like books or don't like the genre you write or don't like your cover or sales description or writing. And it's possible no one will buy your writing, as there are no guarantees.

Also, no matter what you write, other people will judge it and criticize it or you. Readers have different tastes, and no writer pleases all of them.

Mary Higgins Clark's books are so popular publishers have paid her advances above $10 million per book. Yet a member of a book group I belong to sneered at her writing as "trash."

Because you're a reader as well as a writer I'm sure I didn't really need to point out any of that. You knew it. And because you write or want to, I'm guessing you don't believe you can avoid judgment, rejection, or criticism. You know it's part of the deal, yet you still want to write.

So when it comes down to it Fears 4-6 are actually different forms of Fear 7, the fear of feeling like a failure if any of those things happen.

Let's start once again with your definition. If succeeding or failing rests on other people's reactions, you've got limited say over that. Which makes it scarier. We're right back to Fears 4-6.

So why not instead choose a definition that gives you more say over your life?

For instance, if you define failure as failing to try something you want to do, then you can choose whether or not you fail because you can choose to try.

But what if in your heart it matters deeply to you what others think of your writing? Maybe redefining failure feels like semantics. Success means people buying your writing or selling a certain amount or getting rave reviews. Many writers, including me, set all those goals.

The key is not pretending those things don't matter, it's moving forward despite fear.

Just as I didn't let feeling nervous the first time I taught a legal writing class keep me from doing it, you don't need to let fear of failure keep you from writing.

The visualization techniques in Chapter 14 may help. Get relaxed and see yourself writing. Picture yourself at your keyboard, writing in a notebook, editing pages, or holding your finished book.

And in real life you can practice writing when you feel anxious about it. Start with a journal entry or list of favorite movies if you need to. Get used to feeling afraid and writing all the same. Odds are the feeling will fade.

It's also worth (again) becoming aware of the questions you ask yourself. Write out questions designed to ease your transition into writing.

Finally, what I've found most useful is to decide there are no failures, only results. (A view I've seen attributed to many different people, including Tony Robbins.) Most everything we learn in life is a process of doing something that doesn't work, changing our approach, and trying again. Whether it's learning to walk, swim, ride a bike, or write a book that sells, most of us need to "fail" many times to learn.

One of the novels I published, When Darkness Falls, fits within a genre I don't otherwise write. (Paranormal romance/gothic horror.) While if I offer it free for Kindle it gets some downloads, it rarely sells. It took two years before it earned back what I spent paying a service to convert it for Kindle and for a cover. Unlike with my other books, so far the advertising I've tried hasn't done much to move the needle.

I could see it as a failure.

But instead I value what I learned from it. It was the first book I published in paperback using the KDP dashboard. It's the only novel I have in Amazon's KDP Select program, so I use it to try out Kindle Countdown deals and free days. It's also a good book to advertise on other ad platforms because any sales I do see almost certainly result from the ad.

Also, it's a book I wrote before my bestselling Awakening supernatural thriller series, though I published it after. I see a progression in my writing from that book to the Awakening series to my newest suspense/mystery series.

For a non-writing example, I once told my brother Keith, who has loved taking photos all of his life, how my favorite photos of myself (and pretty much anyone else) were ones he took. I asked him how he did it.

He said, "You don't see the thousands I throw away."

This was back when all photos were taken on film, meaning he spent money on the film and the processing for each one. He could easily have viewed all those thrown-out photos as failures and let that stop him. But if he had, he'd never have produced so many images that have made so many people happy.

He also wouldn't be the excellent photographer he is today.

Before moving on to Part 3, which covers redesigning the world around us, here are some questions to help you move forward in the face of fear:

*W*hat's a pattern interrupt you can use if you start obsessing about what others will think about your writing?

_____

_____

*W*hat questions can you create to help you find time to write?

_____

_____

_____

*H*ow do you imagine you'll feel if you if you start your most important writing project?

_____

_____

_____

. . .

*I*f you finish it?

_____

_____

_____

*W*ho in your life makes you feel encouraged about your writing?

_____

*L*ist 3 three things you can do to spend more time interacting with that person.

_____

_____

_____

*I*f your friend wanted to write a novel and was struggling with getting started, what advice would you give?

_____

_____

_____

*R*ead 3 critical reviews of a book you love. What did you learn from the reviews?

_____

_____

. . .

*D*id you agree with the criticisms?

_____

_____

*W*hat would you say to that author about the reviews?

_____

_____

_____

Part Three

CREATING AND RECREATING THE WORLD WE LIVE IN

Chapter Sixteen

SOMETIMES IT'S NOT YOU

…we decide for ourselves what makes us happy. This requires an act of supreme kindness to ourselves….[happy people] don't dance to the happiness messages other people send them: buy this product, join this club, follow this ideology.

- Rick Foster & Greg Hicks, *How We Choose To Be Happy: The 9 Choices of Extremely Happy People— Their Secrets, Their Stories*

One of the challenges of being someone who tends toward anxiety is figuring out what's about you and what's about the situation you're in.

For years when I practiced law people assured me that every lawyer is anxious. They also told me no matter what job I had, I'd feel anxious because that was just how I was.

For a long time I believed them despite that I'd had jobs where I rarely felt anxious about the work itself. Nor had my previous jobs caused me to lie awake worrying about whether I'd be able to finish all my tasks that day, week, or month or whether I'd make a mistake.

I thought maybe being a lawyer was intrinsically different than every other job I'd done. And I didn't feel anxious all the time. There were plenty of times I had fun at work, and I appreciated that my salary eventually alleviated most of my deepest fears about money.

When I stopped practicing full time and began spending the bulk of my work life writing, though, something amazing happened. I almost immediately began to feel more relaxed. That's so despite that my money concerns are much greater now, as writing so far has been a far less reliable source of income.

I still get anxious, or I wouldn't be writing this book.

But it happens far less often. And person after person has seen me and commented on how much more relaxed I look and seem and how much happier, including people who don't know that I changed my work situation.

If all my anxiety issues were self-generated, I would be equally anxious now.

So it's important to pay attention to the world around us.

We may be able to make changes that help us enjoy life more and feel calmer. Our jobs, the people in our lives, how we spend our time, what we do for fun, all these things and others can significantly affect our quality of life.

For that reason, the following chapters offer some suggestions for interacting with people and the world differently and seeking out people and situations that increase our chances of happiness and calm.

We'll start with getting our of your own head.

Chapter Seventeen

GETTING OUT OF YOUR HEAD

*W*e've talked a lot about what you say to yourself that adds to your anxiety, increases feelings of calmness, and influences happiness. The words you use, the scenes you imagine.

All those are important to how we feel.

But.

It's also important to get out of our heads. As writers, many of us love to analyze. We might find reframing questions and rewriting our experiences fun. Yet sometimes no matter what questions I ask myself, what I visualize, or how many relaxation exercises I do, I'm stuck in anxious thoughts.

As a writer, full-time or not, you also probably spend a lot of time alone and in your own head. To add to the alone time these days much of our interacting with other people, including writers and readers, is done online.

If you're an introvert, at first this may sound great, as it did to me. But when I started working and writing mainly from home, I quickly found that being alone all the time (I also live alone) could lead to feeling blue and uneasy.

It gives me a lot of time to cycle through everything I might worry or feel sad about.

In contrast, getting outside or being around other people necessarily requires me to look outward and pay attention to other things.

Now I make a point to be sure I've got at least two or three things scheduled where I interact with other people during the week, and a couple things each weekend. The activities aren't expensive. Sometimes it's meeting another writer or a friend from my law firm days for a cup of tea or to take a walk. Also, part of why I teach is that it builds interaction into my schedule.

So if you find yourself struggling, don't forget to look at how much time you're spending alone and/or how much time you spend thinking. Talking to someone else in person or going out your door will likely do more to shift your mood than you expect.

In addition, the world we live in influences how we feel. As much as what we say to ourselves and focus on affects our moods so do interactions with other people, our jobs and careers, and the environment in which we live.

Just as we create a world for our characters we can do our best to create a world for ourselves that increases our happiness and peace of mind. Sure, it's not like writing where we get to choose everything about it to suit our story. In fact, some days it feels like we can't choose anything.

But to the extent we can why not create a life, a world, with the aim of being happy and calm?

Let's start with our environment.

Chapter Eighteen

DESIGNING YOUR ENVIRONMENT

*F*eeling happier is not only about what thoughts your brain generates or what you feed your mind. It's what surrounds you and what you experience.

As I'll talk about in Chapter 20, we can choose to spend more time with people who help us feel our best and look at life in its best light or who help us move toward where and who we want to be. First, though, let's start a little closer to home.

LISTENING TO YOUR SENSES

In writing, drawing on all five senses creates a more vivid experience for the reader. In life, being aware of all your senses allows you not only to choose what remains most vivid in your memory but to experience more of what improves your mood and overall well-being.

It's not a cure-all, and you may still feel anxious at times. But you will likely have more hours when you feel calm and happy than you did before.

SOUNDS

How do certain sounds make you feel? And how much sound is enough? Too much?

Paying attention so that you can answer these questions can make your life more peaceful and joyful.

Some people love the stimulation of noise around them. They flip on the TV as soon as they walk in the door and leave it on whether they are talking, eating, reading, or working.

I find that stressful.

If I'm watching a show or movie or listening to audio, I want to pay attention to it. Having those things playing in the background while I'm trying to do anything other than a routine, mindless task makes me tense.

That doesn't mean I never use background sound. As I talked about in Chapter 5, I sometimes use audio to occupy parts of my mind and block anxiety.

Even with that, though, I need to be careful. If I play audio more than an hour or two each day for a few days, it adds to my stress.

After my parents' deaths, I became so noise sensitive it felt almost physically painful to hear loud sounds like car horns or the construction drilling across the street from where I lived. Later I realized I'd had the radio or TV on almost all the time when I was home and I'd overloaded myself with sound to block out all the painful feelings.

So even when I think I don't want it, I need a certain amount of quiet. These days if I start feeling tense I take a quick mental survey of how much sound I've had around me.

On the other hand, some sounds soothe me.

Quiet classical music. Rain, thunder, or bird songs on a CD or in real life. My parakeet chirps away much of the day, and I like that. And I like white noise, so the hum of my air cleaner or of the trains outside the window relaxes me.

Your reaction to sounds may be different from mine, but there are almost certainly some that make you feel calmer and others that stress you.

*O*ver the next two days notice how you feel when certain sounds continue and how your body reacts.

_____

*I*s there a type of music that causes your muscles to relax? _____

*T*hat makes you feel cheerful? _____

*G*ets you energized and ready to go do something?

_____

*D*o you like background noise? _____

*W*hat kind?

_____

. . .

*A*re there nature sounds that relax you? _____

*W*hich ones?

_____

_____

*E*xperiment with sounds and see what relaxes you, stresses you, or makes you feel full of energy, hopeful, or happy.

SIGHTS

Studies show that looking at nature or, if you can't get out into nature, a photograph or drawing of it relaxes most people. Nature is one example of a sight that may help you feel calmer or happier.

I also feel calm, for whatever reason, when I walk along a sidewalk in downtown Chicago surrounded by tall buildings. Something about skyscrapers and hundred-year-old buildings that are still standing gives me perspective on my life and makes me feel more relaxed.

Some people may like looking at pictures of kittens or parakeets (okay, maybe that one is just me) or sunsets or amusement parks.

Whatever sight makes you relax and feel good, why not find a photo, print, or painting of it and put it up on your wall or somewhere where you'll see it first thing in the morning?

You can also choose images for your laptop or phone, but it's good to have something you can see without turning to an electronic device.

Colors also can affect how you feel.

My writing office at home has apricot walls. It might not be for everyone, but it helps me feel more cheerful in the middle of winter and it helps me relax in the summer. The color reminds me of sunrises or sunsets.

O ver the next two days notice the colors in whatever room or place you're in. Which ones help you feel happy?

A re there any colors that make you feel sad or stressed?

W hat sights do you enjoy?

I f you could wake up in your favorite place what would you see first thing in the morning?

SMELLS

Most of us are so used to watching movies and television that we think mainly of what we sense with our eyes and ears. But smell, taste, and touch can be key both to vivid writing and to a happy life.

In addition, smell is closely linked to memory.

If you pay attention to what different scents make you remember you can choose the ones that remind you of happy or peaceful moments.

Also, whether linked to memory of not, many of us react strongly to different smells.

Citrusy scents with hints of lemon or orange (or actual lemons or oranges) help me feel upbeat and happy. The smell of cooking food or baking relaxes me, mainly because for so many years I never had time to cook at home.

For pure relaxation, I love lavender, vanilla, cinnamon, and, especially, chocolate. The last one is probably because I find hot cocoa to be a very calming drink.

Other smells are migraine triggers for me or otherwise make me feel ill, such as almost any flowery perfume or detergent.

In fact, if you have allergies, asthma, or other breathing difficulties, the scent you may need could be no scent. You may need to look for unscented detergent, soap, shampoo, etc. and/or buy a good HEPA air filter. I love the clean smell of the air — which is really a nonscent — when my filter is going full blast.

Similarly, if artificial scents cause you problems you may want to seek out the sources of natural scents like fresh oranges or lemons, cocoa, or flowers.

The smells of fresh grass and leaves help me relax and lift my mood, as does the scent of the ground right after it rains. In the fall, spring, and summer, I walk out of my way to spend time in Chicago parks for that reason.

Other outdoor smells affect me too.

I love the smell of caramel and cheese popcorn wafting out of Garrett's Popcorn. (This is an outdoor smell in Chicago, trust me. I won't mention the unpleasant street odors, of which there are many.)

As you notice how you respond to scents, pay attention to what relaxes you, energizes you, or excites you. Once you're aware, you can help your body relax or help yourself feel upbeat by seeking out the right scents for you.

Caveat:

If you live with someone else you'll need to take that person's sensitivities and feelings into account. But hopefully you can find a scent that works for you both or find some small space where you can indulge in the scents that make you feel the best.

*R*emember a particularly happy time. Are there scents you remember from it?

_____

_____

*C*an you bring those scents into your life more often?

_____

*W*hat scents, if any, make you feel unwell?

_____

_____

*L*ist two scents that help you feel more relaxed.

Where can you find them?

TASTE

As with smells, which are closely related to taste, the key with what tastes help you feel your best is experimenting.

Note not only the momentary feelings but shifts in mood that last. For example, a glass of wine can help me feel more light-hearted if I'm worried about something, but if one glass leads to two or three I'm more apt to dwell on whatever I'm anxious or unhappy about and feel sad or angry. So I'm better off reaching for a comforting hot cocoa to soothe myself or a glass of orange juice with ice to spark my energy.

Also, I find it useful to save both smells and tastes as a treat rather than overloading.

If you always scent the air in your home with vanilla, eventually your brain will block it out. Likewise, if I drink a cup of hot cocoa every day, it'll stop being a taste that leaves me feeling warm and relaxed and turn into a daily routine I barely notice.

Similarly, I like cola, but there's so much sugar I don't want to drink it all the time. I don't care for diet soda and my stomach reacts badly to it. So once in a great while, usually when I'm taking a day off work, I have a real Coke or Pepsi. Because it's rare, every time it makes me feel like I'm on vacation.

Taste raises the issue of disorders specific to eating or drinking alcohol. Those issues, as well as substance abuse, plague

many people. Dealing with them is beyond the scope of this book.
If you feel you may have issues, though, please reach out for help.

*O*ver the next week notice how you feel both when you eat
certain foods and for an hour or two afterwards.
What are your go-to tastes if you're feeling low?

----

*H*ow do you feel when you eat them?

----

*H*ow do you feel an hour or so later?

----

*W*hich tastes make you feel happy?

----

*D*o you still feel good an hour or two later?

. . .

f not, try substituting a different food and see if the good feelings last longer.

o the same for tastes that help you relax.

TOUCH

As with the other senses, you can find out what sensations relax you, energize you, or leave you feeling happier by paying attention to your body, your thoughts, and your mood.

Evaluating touch came easy to me because, fortunately or unfortunately, my skin is very sensitive. Some fabrics cause hives, others itching. It's hard for me to wear anything with wool in it unless it's over other clothes, so a coat might be okay, but not a sweater that lies directly on my skin.

The upside of that is I'm also very aware of what feels good.

Fleece makes me feel warm and relaxed. Because of that, I have a thick fleece blanket on my couch for winter and I own multiple fleeces to wear under coats when I go outside or to keep me warm inside.

Also, generally, I feel best when I'm warm. Being cold makes me feel blue and also anxious.

It's part of why I became a tea drinker. I don't like coffee — too bitter — but I love holding a warm mug and drinking a warm drink. For over a year I had braces and couldn't drink hot drinks with them in, so sometimes I heated a mug of water and held it as I read or watched TV. It helped me relax.

You may feel more relaxed in a cooler environment or find the layers I tend to wear constricting. Likewise, while I find getting a massage once a month lessens my anxiety (so much so that I'll cut most other expenses before that), you may be uncomfortable with a massage therapist digging into your muscles.

The key is figuring out what helps you relax and feel happier and looking for ways to bring more of it into your life.

*D*o you feel better if you're in a warm climate or a cool one? _____

*D*oes the sun on your skin feel good or too hot?

_____

*D*oes humidity make you feel closed in or help your muscles unwind? _____

*W*hat fabrics feel best on your skin?

_____
_____

*W*hat physical sensations help you relax?

_____
_____

*I*ncrease your energy level?

_____
_____

Chapter Nineteen

WORDS WITH PEOPLE

You are the average of the five people you spend the most time with.

- Jim Rohn

$\mathcal{O}$ur environment also includes other people.

When I feel particularly anxious or discouraged, I often struggle with how to talk to others. On the one hand, we all need to be able to share our fears and concerns. As I'll talk about more in Chapter 21, it's important to have friends to confide in.

Yet I don't want to be that person who does nothing but complain or who stresses other people out by spilling all my anxieties over and over. It's not good for relationships. Much as (I hope) your friends and family want to support you, they also want to connect with you in other ways. And they need you to listen to them, too, not make it a one-way street.

Also, just as ruminating silently in our own minds can increase our anxiety, so can doing the same thing aloud with another person.

All of the above are reasons why most of us need to know how to put on the brakes or shift the conversation once we've told others once or twice (or twenty times) about how worried or discouraged we feel.

CHANGING YOUR TOPICS WHILE BEING YOURSELF

Talking about other things can be a challenge if all that's in your head and heart right now are things you're worried or unhappy about.

You may feel as if you're lying, or at least not being your real self, if you try to put on a happy face or talk about how great things are. Or that may take too much energy. Or you might truly feel unable to think of anything else to say.

If that's where you are (and I have been there more than once), try thinking of it not as pretending to be someone you're not but as choosing a path to help yourself feel better and have stronger relationships.

Just as you might exercise or eat differently if you were training for a marathon (I'm guessing here — I'm in no way a runner), you may speak differently when aiming for a calmer, happier life.

WRITING THE DIALOGUE

Much as you plan scenes between your characters, you can imagine in advance some dialogue prompts for when you're feeling particularly anxious or are having trouble thinking about anything but your worries.

Below are some approaches I've used.

As with everything in this book, you need to see what works for you and what doesn't, so choose what you feel might be most helpful. Or create your own prompts.

- **Ask the other person what that person feels good about, happy about, or grateful for right now.**

This type of question can break what often becomes a mutually self-defeating cycle in conversation.

Many people have a tendency to match anxious with anxious, sad with sad, discouraged with discouraged, which can mean you both feel worse after talking. Also, some people compete to say who had a worse day, week, boss, in-law, etc.

Raising a more upbeat topic shifts the focus for both of you and breaks that cycle of one-upping the other on hard times.

Also, asking this type of question can ease the mind of your friend (or partner, colleague, or family member). That's because most of us don't feel right going on about good things in our lives if the person we're talking to feels down. Asking what's going well for your conversation partner lets that person know that even if you're going through hard times you still want to share in their joy.

There may be times, however, when it's hard to hear what's terrific in someone else's life. That may make you feel worse.

If that's how you feel right now, here's a different option:

- **Say that you're going through a tough time right now, but rather than talk about it you'd like to focus on something else, such as a mutual interest.**

That interest could range from something very personal, like happier times you and the friend shared, or more general, like a sports team or hobby you're both enthusiastic about.

And here's a related approach:

- **With or without mentioning that you're going through a hard time, ask something that helps you learn more about the other person. You can ask about favorite vacations, family history, or details about work that you've never delved into before.**

The classic *How To Win Friends And Influence People* by Dale Carnegie introduced me to this approach.

I read it when I was feeling my worst after my move home from California. (Are you seeing a theme here? I've got nothing against California, seriously. It's just a good shorthand way of referring back to that time.) The strategy of asking others about themselves relieved me from saying how badly I felt my life was going.

As a plus, I learned a lot about the people around me.

Not only that, but to my surprise I moved from being someone with one or two close friends who was uncomfortable meeting new people to being someone others sought out and enjoyed being around. I began to have fun meeting new people and felt far more confident in my ability to start a conversation.

The confidence came not because I became more interesting, but because people love to talk about themselves. It's a great gift to really listen to them as they share with you what matters to them.

I learned these strategies because I desperately needed a way to interact with people without bursting into tears or cycling through my worries repeatedly. But they resulted in far wider networks of friends, acquaintances, and business colleagues that have made my life richer in so many ways, both professionally and personally.

One other idea:

- **Make a mental list of books, movies, or television shows you've loved or positive current events in the news (you can find them if you look hard enough) or cute photos on social media and choose some to share or talk about.**

The longer the list, the more options you have for upbeat or at least neutral conversation. If your friend doesn't share your taste, ask for your friend's favorites and why.

You may be able to figure out other things to talk about. My list isn't meant to be the only way, but to get you thinking in advance about what to talk about.

*I*magine you are writing dialogue for a character who for whatever reason is not allowed to discuss personal problems or concerns. What would they talk about?

_____

_____

_____

*T*hink of 3 people you talk to regularly who have heard about your anxious or discouraged thoughts pretty often. For each one, think of 3 conversation openers that are likely to lead to happier topics.

_____

_____

_____

Chapter Twenty

CALMER, HAPPIER PEOPLE

As I talked about in Chapter 1, many people's brains don't slip easily into the anxiety groove. Also, some people employ ways of thinking and talking to themselves and others that increase their peace of mind and happiness.

Finding someone like that can help you adopt your own strategies for a healthier, happier life.

I'm not suggesting a modern day equivalent of Pollyanna. We all know people so annoyingly cheerful it gets on our nerves, and whose optimism makes us wonder if they're simply out of touch with reality.

Also, unless you're uncommonly lucky, you've experienced some genuinely difficult things. Someone who simply says "turn your frown upside down" probably won't be all that helpful.

For those reasons, I'm talking about finding someone who has dealt with life's ups and downs, can still focus on what's good in life, and puts challenges in perspective.

My own model for greater calm and happiness is an attorney I'll call Ted.

From when I first got to know him, Ted struck me as a happy person. He enjoys his law practice, does well at it, and has a sense of humor that, most of the time, makes it fun for him. He strives to do his best for his clients, but when he feels he's done that he doesn't second-guess himself. He speaks with pride about his kids, who are now adults, and often remembers good times he spent with them as they grew up.

Not long after I met him he said something like, "Nothing bad has ever happened to me."

I took him at his word and assumed he really hadn't had anything bad happen. And I thought, sure I could be calm and happy if my life were like that.

BAD THINGS DO HAPPEN

Later I learned that Ted is a cancer survivor.

Years before I met him he had surgery and then a long course of chemotherapy. The drugs made him sick and threw off his digestive system so much that he didn't like to be around anyone else when he ate.

Ted also is the same person I mentioned in Chapter 7. He was literally run over by a car while he was mowing his lawn and nearly lost his leg.

He didn't, but for eighteen months, after multiple surgeries, he had to stay off his leg. He first used a wheelchair and then crutches. An attorney who works with only one partner, he worked almost the entire time. His wife had to drive him from courthouse to courthouse and help him into and out of his wheelchair. Later he navigated a Chicago winter on crutches, swinging across ice-filled parking lots with a backpack over his shoulder. Only after extensive physical therapy did he get back into shape.

And it's not as if Ted only ran into serious life events as an adult. When he was only eighteen, his dad died.

With this string of events, all out of his control, Ted would have every reason to feel like life or fate or the gods had it in for him. Or to believe that the world is a dangerous place and fear and worry are the appropriate response.

So how is it that Ted can say nothing bad ever happened to him and mean it?

He chooses what aspects of his life to focus on, keeps perspective, and concentrates on taking action rather than anticipating the worst.

• Focusing On What's Good

When I asked him how he could say nothing bad had happened to him given what he'd been through, Ted told me that he had raised three kids who are now adults. He was able to pay for their college educations. They are all in good health, have good jobs, and are happy. To him, that's nothing bad ever happening to him.

In short, when he sums up his life, he choses to focus on what's great, which includes his children.

Ted also says he's enjoyed every job he's ever had. (He was a police officer and later a prosecutor before being a criminal defense attorney. He also worked summers in a steel mill to pay for college.)

When I string together what he's said about his work in the time I've known him, though, I realize he's dealt with many situations that were stressful, scary, and clearly dangerous in the moment.

But when he tells the stories he emphasizes the humor and what he learned.

• Perspective

Ted also chooses what to say to himself when things go wrong.

If he made a mistake he doesn't beat himself up. He says, "Ah, I shouldn't have done that," or "I learned the hard way," and sets out to do it differently the next time. Rather than agonizing about the discomfort of the moment he laughs in retrospect at his mistakes or embarrassment.

As important, having been through cancer, the car crash, and the loss of his father at a young age, when he's faced with a difficult situation that would send me into serious anxiety, he tells himself that no one has died. He reminds himself that he still has a place to live and a job and family he loves. It puts it in perspective for him.

- ### The Next Step

When facing a challenge, including a life-threatening one, Ted shifts quickly to how best to deal with it.

Much like Anthony Robbins' advice about questions, Ted asks himself things that help him move forward rather than ones that get him stuck in a groove of fear.

At each stage of his cancer, from diagnosis through treatment, he didn't ask himself repeatedly what if the worst happened or why he had been singled out for misfortune.

He said, "What's the next step?"

With his leg, after his brief period of wondering why it happened to him he shifted to how he could get the best possible result.

THE VALUE OF A MODEL

Long before I met Ted I'd started learning and using many of the techniques I've outlined in this book.

I doubt Ted ever heard of any of them. He's not someone who reads self-help books. So far as I know he's never employed a professional life coach or gone to therapy. Yet he naturally adopted most of those techniques. Maybe he learned them from his parents or the people around him in the same way I learned how to be anxious and to worry from my family.

That he didn't need to consciously learn and adopt these techniques, though, makes them no less effective.

Seeing how he defaults to these strategies and how well they work for him reminds me to put them into practice myself. That he hasn't lived a charmed life reassures me. He doesn't deny his experiences or struggles. He will sometimes say how difficult something was. But he spends most of his time and most of his words on what's going well or what he can do to make things better.

Contrary to my fear that letting go of anxiety will undermine my life, without it he's happy and he still spots concerns and addresses them.

Often now when confronted with something that sets my anxiety surging I ask myself what Ted would say. And it helps.

*D*o you know someone who seems generally happy and upbeat in a way that you'd like to emulate? _____

*H*ave you asked how that person handles tough situations? _____

*C*an you ask that person what thoughts work best for staying calm and happy? _____

*I*f you don't know anyone like that, what is one thing you could do this month to expand your circle of acquaintances?

_____

Chapter Twenty-One

FRIENDS WHO UNDERSTAND YOUR ANGST

*F*riends who understand our anxieties and ways of dealing with the world, and perhaps share our struggles to be calm, also can be key to happy lives. With them we feel free to confide our worries or our discouraged feelings and thoughts.

We know they'll understand.

THE GOOD AND THE BAD

There's a sense of ease and relief in being able to share our fears.

Further, in helping friends cope with their concerns, we sometimes see more clearly what we need to do for ourselves. Just as it's easier to spot issues and how to fix them in someone else's writing than in our own, so it is with our friends' worries. That means we can support and help one another and improve our own lives, too.

For example, one of my friends shares my worries about health issues and understands how hard it can be to break free of them.

Last fall I could tell him that I stepped wrong, felt a new pain in the foot that was broken, and feared that I rebroke it. He understood that I knew in my head that the fear was baseless — because I was still walking and not in terrible pain — but that I needed to talk about it rather than dwelling on it in silence.

He also never immediately dismiss my concerns, which often makes me double down on my anxiety to "prove" that something really is terribly wrong.

This kind of support means a lot to me because I have moments or days when everything I've shared in this book simply doesn't work. In those times when I just need to ride it out, it's nice to have a friend who understands. He won't laugh at me or tell me I'm being ridiculous, and he'll sympathize with how anxious I feel.

These same types of friends also can be good ones to do a little research on your behalf. (And you can return the favor.)

Assuming they don't share your same exact fears, they can hunt for the facts you need to address your issue and report them back, filtering out any tangents they went on that might, if you indulged in them yourself, heighten your worry.

While the facts won't necessarily make your anxiety go away you can answer important questions without increasing your fears.

Questions such as:

- Is there a way to get your money back on that purchase?
- Is your injury one that requires an emergency room visit or will a phone call to the doctor on Monday be enough?
- Do you live in a flood plain?

These types of friends, however, also can reinforce our visions of worst case scenarios.

They can encourage us to think about how terrible things are or let us go on indefinitely about our fears.

The good news is that you may be able to help each other.

FRIENDS HELPING FRIENDS

You can seek your friends' help in changing your habits, increasing your happiness, and lessening your fears, and you may be able to help them in the process.

Below are some suggestions on how to do that:

- **Make a pact to limit the number of times you talk about your fears in one conversation without shifting to either a solution or happier subjects.**

For instance, you might agree that if you come back to the same fear, saying the same thing about it, three times your friend will point that out.

On the fourth time your friend will change the subject. That subject change could be accomplished by asking you about a solution, asking what's good in your life right now, or leading you to specific topic that you otherwise usually enjoy talking about.

You will do the same for your friend, assuming your friend wants you to.

- **Set a time limit.**

This is a variation on the previous suggestion.

Agree that if you talk for ten minutes (or fifteen, whatever you decide) about feeling anxious or down without any talk of ways to improve how you feel or solutions it's time to move on. More serious concerns might allow for more time, so be flexible, but commit to a limit that will apply most of the time.

You might write out these rules so that you can refer to them. As in, "Hey, our guidelines say fifteen minutes. You're already at sixteen so at least for today let's switch and talk about something else."

- **Agree to make an observation.**

Maybe you don't want to impose strict rules of limits. Or you try it and it creates too much conflict in your relationship.

Instead you can agree to point out to each other when you are going over the number of times or a certain number of minutes. You can feel free to keep talking, but sometimes it's helpful to have another person tell you how long you've been dwelling on a topic or worry.

I know if I'm feeling particularly anxious I often don't realize I've circled back to the same worry several times or that I've talked about my fear for more than a few minutes.

- **Agree to point out past similar fears or situations that worked out.**

A reminder that we have been through something like this before and survived can be helpful.

In the moment, we're apt to remember only what's worked out badly in the past. Similarly, we may feel sure things have never been this bad before or we've never felt this worried, upset, or sad. Someone else taking us back can help create some perspective and reassure us that we'll get through it.

Though we didn't have any previous agreement about it, my sister-in-law did that for me when I was in law school.

During my last semester I told her how I was afraid that I would not do well on my exams. I felt much less prepared than previous semesters, as I had gone through the break up of a significant romantic relationship. I feared that I hadn't stayed on top of things the way I usually did.

She listened, sympathized, and then pointed out that I had told her the same thing every single semester, minus the break up but with other upsetting or challenging things happening. Nonetheless, every time I'd done well on my exams.

I still wasn't convinced that this time I'd be okay. But it did help me feel less anxious when I realized I'd had this outsized fear every single semester.

Nearly twenty years later, I still think of that. It reminds me that ninety-nine percent of the time feeling intense anxiety or feeling especially low doesn't mean my life suddenly got much worse than it's ever been.

In the next chapter we'll talk about family members. But first:

*W*hich of the strategies above do you think is most likely to be helpful to you when you talk with your friends?

_____

_____

*D*o you think any of the strategies would be helpful for one of your friends?

_____

_____

*W*hich strategies would your friends be most likely to agree to try?

_____

_____

_____

. . .

*L*ist three other ways you and your friends might help each other feel happier and calmer.

_____

_____

_____

Chapter Twenty-Two

FAMILY

*I*n theory, everything in the last chapter about enlisting your friends' support in feeling happier and less anxious also applies to family.

In practice, family can present more challenges. For one, it's not as if we choose our family, at least not our family of origin.

Also, we have more history with family. A comment from a sibling or parent can have a whole different meaning than the same statement made by a friend or acquaintance. Or we may infer a different meaning whether it's there or not

Finally, often we learned anxious thought patterns or behaviors from our family members.

I learned many wonderful things from my mom. I particularly appreciate her daily example of contributing to the world around her by volunteering for causes that mattered to her.

But I also learned from her how to worry. I don't in any way think that she meant to teach me that. It's simply the way that she thought about the world and spoke to herself.

So what to do if family members tend to fan the flames of our anxiety or unhappiness either inadvertently or purposely?

REDEFINE AND REIMAGINE

We can start by revising how we define family and how we interact with family members.

Some ways to do that include:

- Choosing to connect with extended family members — aunts, uncles, great-uncles, cousins once removed — with whom you feel good
- Adding close friends to your definition of "family" and including them in family events
- Suggesting new family traditions, such as donating together to a good cause at the holidays or volunteering together
- Proposing holiday events that revolve around activities rather than conversation, such as playing games, going out to the movies or a sporting event, jogging (not that I'd ever personally choose jogging), or visiting a museum

SPEAKING OF OTHER THINGS

Also, while you can't change the way your family members talk to you, you can change what you say and how you act with them. If your family is open to it you can try some of the techniques above that you've tried with your friends to refocus your conversations.

If not you can make your own effort to change the conversation using questions to do so.

In the November 20, 2018 article *Keeping Thanksgiving Drama Free*, the Wall Street Journal reported on a woman who asks her family members questions on Thanksgiving. Her goal is to help everyone connect. Her questions also are likely to bring forth happy thoughts and feelings. In addition to asking what everyone feels grateful for, she asks each one about "something that went right in your childhood" and how it affects that person now.

Other questions include something brave each person did that year and how family members prefer others to express love for them.

It's also okay to flat out say, "That makes me anxious. Let's talk about something else."

Don't expect an immediate change of subject, however. People tend to stay in their conversational patterns. When that happens, the image of the old-fashioned vinyl record on a turntable helps me once again. Rather than skipping out of a groove, though, you can purposely stay in it.

Every time the family member returns to the topic that makes you feel anxious you can once again say, "I don't want to talk about that" and suggest a new subject. If it happens ten times, you say it ten times. You are a broken record.

The broken record won't create the most exciting conversation. But that's better than a stressful one. Most likely the family member will get tired and go talk to someone who is more willing to engage in anxiety-producing conversations.

CHECKING OUT AND CHOOSING WHAT YOU SHARE

If you can't derail a stressful topic you may opt to listen and nod without taking part in conversation that focuses on things that make you feel anxious or unhappy.

It can help to plan in advance something positive to think about. It's one of those times multi-tasking can be helpful. While everyone else dwells on fears or worries you can plot your novel in your head.

You might also lower your anxiety by choosing what you share about your life and with whom.

Going back to my mom, about a year after I finished college I wrote my first novel and sent it around to publishers. I got a lot of form letter rejections. I was already writing the second novel.

When I mentioned that, my mom said, "Why would you write another novel when nobody bought the first one?"

I don't believe she was questioning my writing skills. She'd been pretty supportive of my choice to major in writing. But my mom's family struggled with money when she was a child. And as an adult, because my dad had to stop working about ten years early due to injury, she'd needed to be a careful money manager to get us by on limited funds. Devoting time to something that wouldn't pay anything in the foreseeable future didn't make sense to her.

Her words, though, hit all my fears that I wasn't a good writer, that I was wasting my time, or that it was simply impossible even if you wrote a good book to make any money writing. As a result I chose not to talk to my mother about my writing again until I got some short pieces published years later.

Similarly, you may opt to avoid sharing some parts of your life with family members whose comments you know will increase your anxiety or unhappiness.

Finally, you may choose to spend less time with someone in your family if that time leaves you feeling more anxious, depressed, or unhappy. You will need to weigh whether that creates greater problems for you. I know it's often not an easy choice to make.

There have been times, though, where I've found taking a few steps back helps me get into a better place and feel happier.

It's not that I don't care about the family member. But I also need to take care of myself.

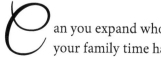an you expand whom you consider to be family to make your family time happier and more peaceful?

. . .

*H*ow?

_____

_____

*A*re there family members whose conversation often leaves you feeling anxious or sad?

_____

*L*ist 3 subjects you feel you could start talking about instead that might interest those family members.

_____

_____

_____

*I*f changing the conversation doesn't work, what are 3 things you could do to stay calm and feel better?

_____

_____

_____

Chapter Twenty-Three

PARTNERS, SPOUSES, SIGNIFICANT OTHERS

Every interaction contains within it the possibility of deep connection with our beloved, with ourselves, and with the cosmos.

— Gay Hendricks, *The Big Leap: Conquer Your Hidden Fear and Take Life to the Next Level*

*I*f you have one person who is your partner, spouse, or significant other that person's emotions, attitudes, and ways of thinking are almost guaranteed to affect you. While in a perfect world our partners would always help us feel calmer and happier, that isn't always the case. Because of that, the same issues that come up with friends and family will likely arise with your significant other at one time or another.

Changing patterns with your partner, though, can be particularly challenging.

On the one hand, our significant others are similar to our friends, assuming it's a relationship we've chosen rather than one imposed on us by society or family obligations.

On the other, if we've made a commitment most of us are more inclined to try to get through difficult times than we might be with a friend. If nothing else, if we're married law and society place barriers in the way of ending the relationship and influence how we define it.

All these factors mean that we may need to be more flexible in our approach.

You may need or want to seek outside help if you're having significant issues. Changing your conversational habits alone isn't likely to fix deeper issues and might spark greater conflict. Or it may reveal other, deeper concerns about your relationship.

If you're otherwise happy with your partner, you may want to review the strategies and approaches in the chapters above and decide which you think would be best. If you think it will be helpful, try talking with your partner about trying out the approaches and why it matters to you.

*O*verall, do you feel your significant other helps you manage any anxiety you have? _____

*H*elps you feel happier? _____

*I*f yes to either, how does that person do that?

_____
_____

*I*f no, what do you feel your partner says or does that has a negative effect on you?

_____
_____

.   .   .

A positive effect?

_____

_____

*W*hat do you do when interacting with your partner that adds to your happiness?

_____

_____

*T*o your anxiety or depressed moods?

_____

_____

*W*hat do you do or say in connection with your partner that increases your joy or sense of peacefulness?

_____

_____

*C*an you do or say whatever that is more often?

_____

*R*eread the chapters on friends and family with an eye toward applying them to your relationship with your significant other.

.   .   .

*H*ave you tried any of these strategies before?

----

*I*f so, how did they work out?

----

*I*f not, which strikes you as most likely to help?

----

*W*hat could you do this week to enlist your significant other in your quest to become calmer and happier?

Chapter Twenty-Four

THE WORLD OF WORK

For most of us a majority of our waking hours are devoted to some type of work, perhaps more than to any other pursuit. (If you're like me, you might devote some sleeping hours to it too. I once dreamed all night about a legal brief I had to write the next day. Boring, I know.)

As I mentioned in Chapter 16, if you feel anxious or unhappy when you work (or where you work) it can be hard to tell whether work is the cause or whether how you feel will follow you wherever you go and whatever you do.

My greater calm and happiness away from a full-time law practice tells me that I wasn't destined to feel significant anxiety no matter where I work or what I do. I still have plenty of concerns as a writer. Some are greater than when I was a full-time lawyer, such as how much I'm earning. Also, being home alone more has meant more time in my own head to spin out negative thoughts.

Short of completely changing your work life to get perspective, which quite often isn't an option, I've found two good ways to figure out how the particular work or job you're doing affects your state of mind:

Method 1: Compare one specific and similar job to another.

Method 2: Break down factors common to all your jobs regardless whether they are similar to one another.

Method 1 worked for me when I had an office job that made me extremely anxious. My direct supervisor gave me great reviews but also frequently yelled, forgot the instructions he'd given me, and changed what he wanted without warning, blaming me for not reading his mind. I had worked similar jobs with the same duties in the past and had felt happy and calm.

Isolating what sparked my anxiety was easy — the four things I just mentioned. Not surprisingly, when I found a different job I felt much happier and calmer.

Comparing job to job didn't work once I became an attorney, though.

As a lawyer I only worked at two places: a large law firm and my own law practice. And the nature of my practice when I went on my own didn't change much, though I had more control.

I had worked as a paralegal for years before law school and done internships as a law student. But at those positions I hadn't had ultimate responsibility for anything. Also, while it hadn't been stressful, I'd become bored at my paralegal job, which was never true as an attorney. I feared high stress was the price I had to pay for work that always kept my mind engaged and challenged me to grow.

It didn't help that almost every attorney I knew felt super stressed. Working in a large firm involved long hours and being pushed to constantly work more, making it hard for most people to wind down whether they had anxiety issues or not.

Those people who were relaxed tended to get fired or disappear pretty quickly because their relaxation often came from not caring if they did a good job or not.

When I started my own firm, at first I eliminated things that increased my stress. But my clients hired me to keep doing the same kind of work I had done in the past. And my fears about not having enough work led me to take on too much. I often felt as if I were on a treadmill that kept speeding up, and at any moment I'd fly off it and crash into the wall. In the long run, in the most significant ways I recreated the atmosphere that I had wanted to leave.

So I still didn't have an answer to whether I felt anxious due to my type of law practice or if it was simply how I was wired. Enter Method 2, looking for commonalities despite differences in jobs.

On first glance, work I did as a temporary secretary wouldn't seem to tell me anything about what I might enjoy as a lawyer. My paralegal work might be closer, but not right on the nose because of the different responsibility level. And while I write a lot as part of my law practice the type of writing and what's needed to succeed are very different than what I do as an author.

All the same, when I looked at specific aspects common to all the work I've done — and particularly focused on what I felt happiest doing — I learned a lot.

The key is to look not at the specific type of work but at the work conditions.

Doing so I discovered I feel happiest, calmest, and most satisfied when:

1. I can focus on major projects for blocks of time of an hour or more (ideally four hours a day) uninterrupted
2. I help other people and can see the impact on them
3. The workplace or at least my own work area is relatively quiet
4. I write
5. I problem solve
6. I feel mentally and intellectually challenged
7. I incorporate public speaking
8. I have enough time off work to spend time with friends and family on a regular basis

9. I earn enough to cover my basic needs and a few luxuries without counting every penny
10. I have enough time away from work that I can read novels regularly
11. I enjoy and have a few moments each day to chat with the people who work with or near me
12. I have control over what work I do and when I do it

While being a lawyer at a large firm and at my own firm scored high on 4-7 and 9, much higher than any other work I ever did, the rest of the points on the list almost never happened. I was lucky to get fifteen minutes without an urgent call or email that demanded my attention, let alone a few hours.

Further, as a lawyer my work didn't allow me to wind down or de-stress often enough.

It was not only the number of hours but the lack of predictability. Whether I scheduled a dinner with a friend or a weekend away, it was always subject to cancellation at a moment's notice. It was a given among lawyers at firms like the one where I started out as an attorney that if you planned lunch, you'd need to reschedule three or four times before both people could actually be there.

When I started my own firm, I followed the same practice, often cancelling my plans or coming back early from vacation even when it wasn't necessary. I adopted the very habits that had made me so unhappy.

I still work on legal cases similar to the ones I did before, but it's on a project basis for another firm. In a month I work fewer hours at law than I used to in a few days. Also, other attorneys manage the case and deal with those late night phone calls or emails. Sometimes that's frustrating, as it means I don't get to make the major decisions. But the trade off is worth it. I can use my legal skills and enjoy the mental challenge, yet I can spend the bulk of my time writing. And when I take time off, it's real time off. No surprise work I'm required to do.

Feel free to look at my list and see if any of the conditions resonate with you. And below are some other factors that affect might affect your anxiety or happiness at work:

- Workspace (office, cube, open plan, factory floor, etc.)
- Nature of co-workers
- Amount of conflict
- Noise levels
- Level of responsibility
- Control over time and duties (or lack of it)
- Physical strain or lack of it
- Regularity of schedule
- Whether schedule matches family's and friends' schedules
- How much contact you have with other people
- The level of team work required or encouraged
- Opportunities or requirements to socialize with coworkers

As you look at these lists and add your own factors do your best to estimate realistically how much of your current work life aligns with what you need to feel your best.

If it doesn't, you can start thinking about changes you might make to increase your peace of mind and work satisfaction. You may try to adjust aspects of your current job, look for a new one, or find ways to apply the techniques in this book to help you feel happier.

The questions below may also help you figure out where you are and where you'd like to be.

·   ·   ·

*O*f the jobs you've held, which one did you feel was the best fit?

_____

*W*hat did you love most about the job?

_____

_____

*W*hat job have you felt most anxious while you're doing?

_____

*W*hat are the common factors between the two jobs?

_____

_____

_____

_____

_____

*W*hat are the differences?

_____

_____

_____

_____

_____

. . .

*W*rite out the characteristics (such as work hours, physical work space, nature of tasks, etc.) of all the different jobs you've held and mark next to each whether you consider that a plus or minus of the job.

----

*D*o you see patterns? _____

*W*hich job features lead to you feeling calmer or happier or both?

. . .

*W*hat features would you like in your ideal job?

----

*W*hat small step could you take today to get more of what you want in your work?

Chapter Twenty-Five

PUTTING IT ALL TOGETHER

The goal in life is not to attain some imaginary ideal; it is to find and fully use our own gifts.

- Gay Hendricks, *The Big Leap: Conquer Your Hidden Fear and Take Life to the Next Level*

$\mathcal{A}$s you change the questions you ask, how you spend your time, and how you interact with others you may encounter some surprises.

While you'll likely feel happier and calmer overall, it's good to be prepared for the moments when you won't. And for how other people may respond to the different choices you make.

OTHER PEOPLE'S REACTIONS

People you once spent a lot of time with may drift away. It's not because they don't care about you or you've done something wrong. And it may not be a conscious choice on their part. They may be disappointed that you won't engage as often in the types of conversations they're used to having. Or they may be in a place in their lives where your shift toward more peace and more happiness makes them uncomfortable.

If this happens you may find out you feel calmer or happier spending less time with this person. Or you may feel sad and abandoned. Or all of those things.

Remember that your friend or family member may return to you later. You can reach out now and then to let the person know you're still around and still care. And/or you may want to devote your time to meeting and connecting with other people, ones who don't expect you to act or feel the way you did in the past.

CHANGES YOU CHOOSE

Feeling better also sometimes prompts you to make changes or gives you energy you lacked before to do so.

As a result, you might be the one who chooses to enter, leave, or alter a relationship. Or you may seek out new job opportunities or create changes within you current job. You might discover new hobbies. You may expand your efforts on your writing or other pursuits.

All of that can be wonderful.

It can also be unsettling.

If you feel overwhelmed occasionally, take a breath. Use the tools you've learned here to feel a little better, then take a look at what's happening. Maybe you'll embrace the change. Maybe you'll take a step back or to one side (metaphorically speaking). There's no right answer. Which is great, because it means there's also no wrong answer.

Experiment. Enjoy. Experience.

WORRY REVISITED

In addition, as you feel calmer and happier, out of nowhere (seemingly) you may begin to worry. You might fear you're missing something important, or that surely things can't be this good.

Likewise, sometimes we experience anxiety or despair in the midst of good times because on some level we fear growing and changing. Feeling fearful or discouraged can be a comfortable place. It's familiar.

In contrast, if we feel good and do all the things we know are most likely to enhance our lives we might just reach great heights. That can be a frightening prospect. We'll have more to lose. We might make bigger mistakes. And so on.

As with the other changes, first do your best to get into a calmer state. Then evaluate what's happening in your life. Often you'll find that nothing's truly wrong. You simply need to get into the habit of feeling better.

If you do need to address a problem or concern, though, you can use questions and other techniques you've learned to do it.

A CALMER, HAPPIER LIFE

I have days and weeks when I feel wonderful. Many more of them than I did ten years ago or even one year ago. Yet sometimes anxiety grips me out of nowhere. (If that weren't so, I probably wouldn't have written this book.)

In fact, the longer I've felt overall calm and happy, the harder it is at first for me to deal with anxiety when it returns. I've often forgotten about or fallen away from the helpful habits and techniques I've learned.

Other times something happens out of my control that seems designed to set off my anxiety. I do everything "right" in response, yet I awaken days in a row feeling anxious. Or I lie awake at night spinning worried thoughts.

In those times, I accept that I may simply feel anxious for a while. I remind myself that I've been here before, and I keep taking small steps and more small steps to feel better.

Eventually it helps. In the meantime, I tell myself that it's okay. I feel anxious, and I'll do my best all the same to go on with life.

Each time I ride out these feelings I'm more able to understand and believe that things are not as bad as they seem at the moment. While I can't stop feeling anxious on a dime (or would we say on a dollar now?), the tools I've shared with you help me gradually shift out of it. This is a big change from when I used to spend weeks or months at a time in that state, certain that I'd never feel good again.

Also, more and more often I feel calm, happy, and excited about life whether or not everything — or anything — is going my way.

I think this is because I've not only learned small ways to improve my mood, I've gained an understanding of what, for me, a happy life includes:

- Time to read extensively
- Seeing the the people I care about often
- New activities
- Public speaking and interacting with others to balance the quiet writing time
- Fun
- Rest
- Projects that absorb my whole mind and heart for hours at a time

Your list will differ from mine, as will the techniques or tools that help you the most.

But if any of the suggestions here help you in your journey toward calm and joy, if any of the insights ring true, I hope you'll embrace them.

And I hope you'll be kind to yourself. The goal is not the perfect life or the perfect you. You are amazing as you are. While one day may be up and another down, you can keep feeling happier and more peaceful month by month and year by year. Good luck and be well.

ALSO BY L. M. LILLY

Super Simple Story Structure: A Quick Guide to Plotting and Writing Your Novel

The One-Year Novelist: A Week-By-Week Guide To Writing Your Novel In One Year

Creating Compelling Characters From The Inside Out

How The Virgin Mary Influenced The United States Supreme Court: Catholics, Contraceptives, and Burwell v. Hobby Lobby, Inc.

As Lisa M. Lilly:

The Worried Man (Q.C. Davis 1)

The Charming Man (Q.C. Davis 2)

The Awakening (Book 1 in The Awakening Series)

The Unbelievers (Book 2 in The Awakening Series)

The Conflagration (Book 3 in The Awakening Series)

The Illumination (Book 4 in The Awakening Series)

When Darkness Falls

The Tower Formerly Known As Sears And Two Other Tales Of Urban Horror

ABOUT THE AUTHOR

An author, lawyer, and adjunct professor of law, L. M. Lilly's non-fiction includes The One-Year Novelist: A Week-By-Week Guide To Writing Your Novel In One Year; Super Simple Story Structure: A Quick Guide to Plotting & Writing Your Novel, and Creating Compelling Characters From The Inside Out.

Writing as Lisa M. Lilly, she is the author of the Q.C. Davis suspense/mystery series, which begins with international best-seller The Worried Man, and of the best selling Awakening supernatural thriller series. She is currently working on The Fractured Man, Book 3 in her Q.C. Davis series.

A member of the Horror Writers Association, Lilly also is the author of When Darkness Falls, a gothic horror novel set in Chicago's South Loop, and the short-story collection The Tower Formerly Known as Sears and Two Other Tales of Urban Horror, the title story of which was made into the short film *Willis Tower*.

www.WritingAsASecondCareer.com
lisa@lisalilly.com

Made in the USA
San Bernardino, CA
23 June 2019